YOUR FEAR OF LOVE

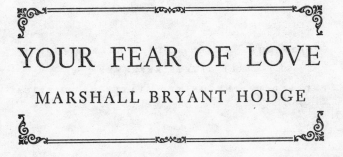

# YOUR FEAR OF LOVE

## MARSHALL BRYANT HODGE

DOLPHIN BOOKS
DOUBLEDAY & COMPANY, INC.
GARDEN CITY, NEW YORK

Lines from "You Always Hurt the One You Love," by Doris Fisher and Allan Roberts. Copyright © 1944 by MCA MUSIC, a division of MCA INC., New York, N.Y. Used by permission.

Biblical quotations, except where otherwise indicated, are from the Revised Standard Version of the Bible, copyrighted 1946 and 1952.

Excerpts from "Getting Ready for Marriage Starts Now," printed in Hi Way, © Westminster Press, April, 1965. Reprinted by permission.

# ACKNOWLEDGMENTS

The scarcity of footnotes in this volume points to my laziness and desire to produce as readable a work as possible, and not to a lack of indebtedness to others. Most of my ideas have been gleaned from innumerable sources, some remembered, some forgotten. This book is the result of the filtering of these ideas through my own experiences.

In addition to many written sources which have influenced me, my experiences and understandings have been profoundly affected by personal contact with colleagues, teachers, and therapists. Notable among these in chronological order of appearance in my life have been: Aaron Ungersma, David D. Eitzen, George R. Bach, Richard A. Hogan, Everett L. Shostrom, Selden B. Marth, Frederick S. Perls, and Walter Kempler. They, of course, are not responsible for the use or misuse I have made of my gleanings.

Every therapist is greatly influenced and changed by his contacts with those who seek his assistance. It is these to whom this book is dedicated. I have drawn extensively from their experiences throughout the book. I have disguised names and details of their lives, of course, so that they cannot be identified. I have learned to be less afraid of love because I have known them. I hope the same has been true for them.

My family has put up with many hours of my absence during my birth struggles with the book. I am grateful to Luella Tate and Margaret Ann Douglas, who spent many hours typing, undangling participles, and healing split infinitives without boring me with the details.

Gratitude is due *Presbyterian Life* for publishing articles in their June 15, September 1, and November 1, 1964, issues, which set in motion the forces behind this book. Many of the ideas which first appeared in that publication have been reworked and appear here in chapters 1, 5, 9, 15, 17.

Some of the material in Chapter 8 appeared in "Getting Ready for Marriage Starts Now," printed in *Hi way*, Westminster Press, April 1965.

# CONTENTS

ance. The Child's Self-acceptance. Parents' Bill of Rights. What Is "Respect"? Underrating Our Children.

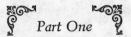

*Part One*

# THE FEAR THAT CRIPPLES US

# OUR FEAR OF LOVE

IT IS WELL PAST midnight when Mike and Helen Brown put down their coffee cups and rise to leave the Schmidts. As they stand by the doorway saying the reluctant good-byes of a delightful evening, Helen feels a sudden rush of warmth and love. Her impulse is to throw her arms around Jane Schmidt and tell her how much their friendship means to her. But just as suddenly the impulse is somehow slightly stifled. Instead, she reaches out, touching Jane's arm lightly, and says, "It's been a wonderful evening!"

While she settles into her seat beside Mike as they drive away, she continues to bask in the glow of pleasure she has felt throughout the evening. "But it's strange," she thinks to herself with vague feelings of disappointment, "that I couldn't show Jane how much I care for her."

At about the same time in another part of the city, Mary Blake calls to her husband, "Jim, aren't you coming to bed now?"

As he goes to the bedroom door and sees Mary already in bed, Jim senses the familiar desire rising within him. "Twelve years married and she's still beautiful," he thinks to himself. And at this moment she looks very inviting.

But Jim's urge to throw off his clothes and jump into bed passes quickly. Instead, he steps to the bed, kisses her tenderly, but without passion, and says, "I'm not really very sleepy yet, honey. I think I'll stay up and watch *The Late Show*."

Leaving the room, he half hopes she will make her invitation unmistakeably explicit, but she only says, "Good night, sweetheart!" and he settles before the television thinking to himself, "Well, if I had gone ahead she might have turned away with an, 'I think I'm just too tired tonight.'"

Mary, meanwhile, turns restlessly in bed for many minutes, filled with sexual desire and the longing to be caressed. She is more disappointed than angry or hurt. "Perhaps I could have told him I wanted him," she thinks to herself, but is surprised to notice a shiver of fear pass through her at the thought of expressing her desire so directly.

It is one of the more puzzling facets of human existence that we often avoid those experiences that we most desire. We long to give and receive expressions of love, but at the critical moment we frequently back away. And in a similar way we frustrate ourselves in many of our strongest desires, such as our wish to be free and spontaneous in our actions.

Our avoidance of longed-for experiences is rooted in fear. We are, as we shall see, afraid of freedom, afraid of sexual enjoyment, and afraid of being ourselves with other people. And the most basic of all these fears is our fear of emotional closeness with others; in a word, love.

Most of us would like to find more satisfaction and less frustration in our personal and family lives. It will help us begin to move in that direction if we can become more aware of our fear of love, the role it plays in our lives, and where it came from. It will also help if we can discover that our other fears are the hand-maidens of our fear of love, aiding and abetting our avoidance of the experience of intimacy.

At first glance the idea that we are afraid to love does not seem to make sense. And while it may not be easy to understand it intellectually, it is even more difficult for many of us to become emotionally aware of this fear within us. Yet there seems to be no better explanation for the fact that moments of feeling very close to another person are rare and short-lived.

Every counselor hears again and again of such moments and the aftermath, which is almost predictable. A husband and wife, for example, may be able to experience an intense flow of love and understanding—perhaps a brief experience including a deeply satisfying sexual experience—but shortly thereafter—sometimes moments later, sometimes the next day—the feeling is gone. Perhaps it is shattered by an argument. Perhaps it slips away as the two seem to withdraw from each other, the closeness replaced by emotional distance. The previous warmth may even appear to have been supplanted by coldness.

## What Is It That Frightens Us?

Why do such experiences occur? The answer appears to be that the experience of love frightens us, even though we may not be aware of our fear.

One young man, John, saw a counselor because he was having difficulties with his wife and in his relation-ships with other people. After some months of indi-vidual and group psychotherapy, he still became in-

dignant whenever it was suggested to him that he
might be afraid of closeness.

One evening when he came to his weekly group-
therapy session the group was depleted because of illnesses and vacations. Only one other member—a
woman named Kathy—was there in addition to him
and the therapist. Often during previous sessions the
group and the therapist had pointed out to him that
almost everything he said was in the form of questions.
It was repeatedly suggested that his perpetual ques-
tioning was a defense against emotional intimacy,
since it allowed him to participate by talking while
revealing practically nothing of himself and his own
feelings. John stoutly maintained that this was not
true and that he used the question technique merely
because he was "objective," took a "scientific approach
to life," and that this was his way of obtaining information that might be helpful to him.

On this particular occasion, however, the therapist
did not allow John to end matters with this explanation. Instead, he was asked to talk directly to Kathy.
He was told he could say anything to her that came
into his mind, except that any question must be re-
phrased into a statement. And so, probably for the first
time, John began to talk directly to Kathy. And, although the things he was saying did not seem particularly significant, he began almost at once to report
that he was experiencing fear. He said he felt cold and
shaky.

During these moments, he was sitting across the
room from Kathy. At that point the therapist asked
him to pull his chair forward until he was directly opposite her, their knees almost touching. He was asked
to continue talking to her. Immediately John began to
experience even more fear. He felt himself begin to

perspire and his legs started aching. When he was asked what his legs wanted to do, the reply was immediate and forceful: "They want to run!"

This fear of closeness John felt so intensely is present in all of us, although some of us are less frightened than others. And if we can become aware of the fear of intimacy within ourselves, a good deal will have been accomplished, for awareness of ourselves and of our fear of love is a step in the direction of emotional health because it opens the door to the possibility of dealing creatively with the fear rather than being blindly enslaved to it.

Why does emotional closeness to others frighten us? The explanation lies in the fact that *caring always involves vulnerability*. When we open ourselves and permit another person to know that we love him, we risk being hurt. And because we know how it feels to be hurt, this risk is frightening.

Everyone has probably experienced feelings similar to those of a woman in the throes of marital difficulties who says, "I don't ever want to care for anyone that much again! It just hurts too much." The vulnerability of the lover is inescapable in every sphere of human relationships. If some tragic misfortune occurs and a child in our family is killed or seriously injured, we suffer deeply, much more than if it were a child down the street whom we scarcely know.

On a somewhat less intense level, a schoolteacher begins to care for children in her classroom. Her love has its satisfactions, but there are also hurts as some children seem unwilling or unable to respond to her interest in them and their welfare.

So striking is the relationship between love and vulnerability that it can be stated almost mathematically. The closer we are emotionally to another human being and the more openly we express our caring, the more open we are to the possibility of being hurt by that person and the more intensely the hurt will be felt. And it is this possibility that frightens us and keeps us wary about establishing close relationships.

The probabilities are that we *will* experience some of the hurt that we fear when we risk love. If we establish significant and close relationships, we will sometimes be disappointed by those we love. If we share confidences, we will sometimes be betrayed. If we count on people, they will sometimes let us down. If we express warmth, others will sometimes seem indifferent or even cold.

It works the other way, too, of course. It is inevitable that we will sometimes hurt those who love us, even though we also love them. Sometimes we will be fully aware of what we are doing and yet seem unable to stop ourselves. At other times we will not recognize, at the moment at least, the fact that we are inflicting hurt.

What it comes down to is that all of us appear unable to enjoy very long periods of closeness. The vulnerability of it is so frightening that one or the other of us finds some way of interrupting it. At such times it is almost as though at some deep level of our beings we find it necessary to say, "Sooner or later I'm going to be hurt by this one whom I love, therefore I must hurt first!"

### Keeping Emotionally Distant

Our fear of emotional intimacy is such a pervading factor in our existence that it has tremendous influence on our personalities and our relationships with others. This is true because *we most often express our fear of love by maintaining emotional distance from others.*

Many symptoms of personality illness appear to serve the purpose of achieving and perpetuating this distance. In one form of severe emotional illness, for example, the patient will remain for hours at a time in one position. Often the position is unusual and even grotesque, almost as if he were saying, "I am different, I am unapproachable." If you *did* speak to such a person there would probably be no visible response. And you might have the eerie feeling at that moment that you were and you were not in the presence of another person. In a way you would be right, for such an individual has gone about as far as possible to absent himself emotionally from others. The fear of closeness with its risk of hurt is so intense that he has built an almost impenetrable wall between himself and the world.

Most of us have not suffered so much emotional damage that we have had to go to such extremes to remain distant from others. But we have all experienced enough hurt and are sufficiently frightened that we build walls of one kind or another between ourselves and others.

Churches often provide illustrations of wall-building on an institutional level. No doubt one reason many people are attracted to churches is that they hope to experience the love for each other that religion talks about. Yet the church frequently appears bent on creating only the appearance of helping people to know each other.

So John and Jane Smith, newcomers to the community, may sit for many weeks in church services among strangers who nod self-consciously to the Smiths and to each other as they leave at the end of the hour. They may attend church suppers or couples' groups and discover that they learn only the most banal super-

ficialities about those around them. They may become
involved in activities and committee meetings and find
that they are mostly business and that the pleasant
chats before and after meetings center around safe top-
ics—jobs, vacations, sports, the children. So churches,
which are made up of individuals, of course, seem at
least as frightened as the rest of us in doing anything
to break through our walls of isolation despite the
skill with which they may depict our need for love.

One young mother discovered how much hurt love
could involve when her two-year-old son was struck by
an automobile while crossing the street in front of
their home. He received head injuries and his breathing stopped for several moments before artificial respi-
ration by the father was effective. These injuries resulted in some impairment in the boy's mental and
physical abilities for several years, causing the parents
much anguish and concern. Some years later, while in
psychotherapy, the mother revealed that following the
accident she tended to withdraw from her children.
She was aware that she was not "letting herself go" in
her expressions of love, but was holding herself somewhat aloof. She said, "I just couldn't stand the thought
of being hurt that much again, so I didn't let myself
get as involved." Through psychotherapy she became
aware of how much satisfaction she was denying herself and her children and was able to bridge the walls
she had so laboriously built.

So important is this wall-building in our lives that
much will be said of the various ways we have of
separating ourselves from others. For the moment it
will suffice to give two common examples.

*Some Ways We Build Walls*

All of us probably engage to some extent in the wall-building device of storing up resentments. Someone irritates us, but we do not express our resentment—at any rate not *all* of our anger. That would be very direct and open, and therefore much too frightening. Instead we cling to our resentment like a long-lost brother, storing it away so we can feel sullen when we are in danger of recognizing and expressing our love for the person. Many a woman, for example, has clung to knowledge of an extramarital infatuation on the part of her husband and used it in this way for years. And whenever he says, "I love you!" she can reply, "Well, you should have thought of *that* before you fooled around with *that* woman!"

The "martyr role" is another very efficient way of building walls. One college student's mother was a master at it. He left for school each morning, not bothering to tidy up his room, because he was content to live amid some disorder. Each day his mother went in and straightened and cleaned it. When he returned in the evening, she reminded him with wounded voice of her sacrifice and how he "could at least show some appreciation after causing me all that work." Then the boy, when he played by the rules of the game, would feel guilty about his "dereliction of duty" and his unexpressed anger about her "martyrdom." For who has a right to feel angry at such a "self-sacrificing" mother?

The effect of this daily household drama was to keep both of them in a constant state of tension in their relationship with each other. As long as they could perpetuate this ritual, they were quite safe from experiencing and expressing their love for each other, love that must have been quite frightening to both of them.

Every marriage counselor is familiar with the "he loves me, he loves me not!" games that men and women often play. Every bit of negative behavior on the partner's part is interpreted as evidence of the lack of love. A husband may react to a cluttered house with the feeling, "If she really loved me, she would do her share and keep the house picked up. It's the least she could do!" A wife may feel, "He must not love me very much. He's constantly forgetting anniversaries and other things he knows are important to me."

Or we may be critical of the quality of our own love by using similar standards. "Surely, if I really loved him," we may say to ourselves, "I would be more considerate of his feelings" . . . or "more sexually responsive" . . . or "more tolerant of his kooky friends."

Such "tallying up" of evidences of love is usually completely meaningless, for it is based on the unreasonable assumption that when we love a person we act that way. Unfortunately we human beings are not so rational as all that! For to express love is frightening to us.

One woman had been separated from her husband for a number of weeks when she appeared at her weekly therapy session with an account of new developments in her relationship with her husband. She said, "He was back home every night this week. Then about the middle of the week we had this big argument. But for the first time when I've really gotten angry, he didn't walk out on me. And when it was over, we began to feel pretty close to each other.

"And that frightened me when I began to see that things might really work out for us. I guess I'm afraid to let myself get involved with him again for fear I'll just get to enjoying it and he'll walk out again. So, do you know what I did? I've just now figured it out. I went back into the past and dug up all kinds of stuff that I could bitch at him about. Just to foul things up, so I wouldn't let myself or him know how much I love him!"

Judging by our behavior, one might begin to conclude that our love ebbs and flows like the ocean. And yet caring is surely not that unstable a quality. Love does not come and go, but our *experience* of love and our *expression* of love is intermittent. And the satisfying moments of giving and receiving love are followed by times of withdrawal of one kind or another, because the experience of love is frightening. To see how it came to be so frightening, we will need to take a look at our childhood experiences.

# II

# THE CYCLE OF REJECTION

ALTHOUGH THERE ARE many theories concerning personality development, there is rather general agreement on at least one important point—the significance of early family life. The emotional environment created by parents (or parent substitutes) is of crucial importance. And although there may be great disagreement as to details, there is general consensus that in families that are relatively healthy in their emotional attitudes, children generally develop a high degree of their potential, while in relatively unhealthy families children are likely to realize less of their potential and often tend to develop personality problems.

Thinking in opposite extremes is always risky, and so it is here. There are, of course, no completely healthy or unhealthy families. Rather we might think of a long line or scale along which families could theoretically be placed as relatively healthy or unhealthy. And no family would be found at either extreme.

This discussion will probably be most meaningful to us if we think of it as it applies to our own personal lives. For most of us it will be helpful to think of ourselves in two roles. One role is that of one's own childhood: "What effects did the family situation in which

I lived as a child have upon my personality? How are these influences affecting my relationships with other people, including my own family, now?"

The second role that might well be kept in mind is our relationship to our children (or future children): "Am I emotionally equipped to be an effective parent? How can I become better able to meet the emotional needs of my children?"

While it is important to see that our childhood family had a profound influence on our present degree of maturity, which in turn will have a great deal to do with the quality of our relationships with our children, it is also important to know that we _can_ change and reach higher levels of maturity. If this were not true, there would be little purpose in discussing personal and family life; and the future would look bleak indeed.

Every family tends to develop repeated patterns of behavior. The parent will do something to which the child responds in a certain way. Often the parent then reacts to the child's response by repeating his original action in an even more forceful way. Like a snowball rolling downhill, this circular pattern gains size and momentum with each repetition of the cycle. One is tempted to use the phrase "vicious circles" in regard to many of these patterns, for it is most easy to see them in operation in negative aspects of personality development and in the growth of our fear of love, but as we shall see later there can be healthy cycles also.

Unhealthy cycles begin with feelings of rejection in family life. Since parents are the primary influence in the family, it is basically the relationship of children with their parents that is under consideration, even though children often feel rejected by brothers or sisters. It can be safely assumed, however, that in early childhood the existence of such feelings can be traced back to the parents, for it is they who establish the emotional tone of the home.

## The Feeling of Rejection

It is no accident that the phrase "feeling of rejection" rather than simply the word "rejection" is used. There is an important distinction, for while it can be shown that children often experience feelings of rejection it often remains a question whether the rejection really exists. There are probably few parents who are so hostile and unfeeling in their relation to their children that they do not *want* to express feelings of affection. More often parents are crippled by personality problems, are frightened of their love, and so are unable to communicate their love freely. So they behave toward their children in ways that appear to be rejecting. Unfortunately, feelings of rejection are damaging even though the parent does not mean to be rejecting.

Two important things need to be said about the feelings of rejection that children experience. First of all, every child experiences some feelings of rejection from parents or, in those instances where the child is not reared by his natural parents, from those who become substitute parents and who are primarily responsible for the child's early experiences. A child reared in an orphanage and foster homes, for example, may have a frequently changing series of "parents," a process that in itself may feel like abandonment and rejection to the child.

✓ But whatever our family circumstances were, each one of us experienced some of these feelings of rejection, and our children will experience some from us. This is only to say that no parent is perfect. As we discuss these cycles of rejection we are talking about all of us, and we are talking about our children. The degree to which children feel rejected will vary, of course, for parents differ in their maturity and in their ability to express love. But every one of us is involved, for feelings of rejection are part of the universal dilemma of being human and rearing children in an imperfect world.

✓ Secondly, there are many kinds of rejection that children encounter. Perhaps the most easily recognizable is that which is accompanied by open hostility toward the child. Most of us have known parents who could not speak to a child without speaking in anger. One such couple seemed unable even to call their children in from playing in the backyard without using a tone of voice seething with hostility. Such parents are often overly severe in punishment and no doubt take out on the child their feelings of frustration in other areas of life. More basically, they are so frightened of genuine emotional involvement that they seem unable to experience their love for their children.

## The Overprotective Parent

Other parents may be too restrictive of a child's freedom, betraying their only slightly disguised hostility. One mother, for no apparent reason, forbade her four-year-old from leaving his yard or playing with other children on the block. Such stern and unnecessary limitations on a child, sometimes bordering on cruelty, tend to choke out the child's ability to be spontaneous and open in his activities.

These rather direct forms of rejection are hard for a child to handle. He is confused by all the hostility coming his way, for he does not know what he has done to deserve such treatment, since in fact he has *not* deserved it. These experiences are particularly damaging, of course, if they are not offset in part by genuine expressions of love by the parents.

While these forms of rejection are very difficult for the child, there are others that are as emotionally crippling. Perhaps they are even harder for children to cope with because they are subtle and are disguised as expressions of love. Often they involve some form of overprotection on the part of parents, and tend to prevent the child from becoming an individual in his own right.

Parents who place a great deal of emphasis on religion may be particularly prone to overprotective forms of rejection. Often they feel that the direct expression of anger is wrong; so they do not get angry at the children, but, without realizing it, they express their hostility in subtle ways such as overcontrolling the child's life. These parents may also be frightened about the dangers they feel exist for the child if he is allowed unrestricted contact with other children and adults who are not part of the religious community. As a result, they may limit the child's opportunities to learn and grow through encountering people of diverse backgrounds.

These masquerades of love have sometimes been called "smother" love (as distinguished from mother love) because they tend to smother the child in his attempts to become a person. For one man, Ron, this symbol of smothering appeared to become the central psychological fact of his life. Ron sought the help of a psychotherapist because he was having difficulty in his marriage. In the first session he described his relationship to his mother as being "very warm and close." As he talked further, however, it became evident that his mother had used this "closeness" to control him as a child and that she had in this way kept him very dependent upon her, thereby rejecting his right to be an individual.

Ron remembered that she constantly used such phrases as "You're my boy!" and "I live through you." The implication was always present that he must do nothing to disappoint her or she would be terribly hurt. This device of putting great responsibility on Ron for her well-being worked quite effectively. She did not have to resort to any physical punishment because he made no effort to rebel. He was "mother's boy."

During Ron's childhood years he had a recurring dream that seemed to symbolize the threat to his individuality that his mother's all-enveloping smothering and "loving" domination posed for him. He would dream that he was running down the center of a stadiumlike field, with empty stands on each side of the field. Then he would look up and see that he was suddenly surrounded by great blobs of a heavy, sticky, molasseslike substance, reaching higher than his head and closing in on him from all sides. He would wake up from this terrifying dream just as he was being engulfed by this mass of goo, which threatened to smother him.

When Ron finished telling this dream and was asked what thoughts came to his mind in relationship to the idea of being engulfed, the things he mentioned seemed to corroborate the idea that even as a young man he still feared his individuality would be smothered. He first mentioned that engulfment suggested boot camp in the Marines, where he had felt engulfed. He said, "There was no time there for me to think for myself. I couldn't escape—I was being controlled!"

When asked about further thoughts on the subject, he said, "I always think of death in terms of smothering." He also reported that he always had a panicky feeling in crowds of people, a feeling of being engulfed and smothered.

All of these reactions seem to tie in with the fear of smothering and of being pushed around, so to speak, psychologically. All of Ron's life up to that time was crippled by the curtailment of his experiences through the very subtle means of overprotection by his mother, who constantly expressed concern that he be dressed warmly enough, who limited his activities with his friends lest he become too tired, and who was always preoccupied with her insistence that he do the "right" things.

Another man, Dan, was crippled emotionally by a mother who answered his every wish as a child. This is another subtle counterfeit of love that conceals underlying hostility, for by this means Dan's mother kept him very dependent on her. She had not wanted him in the first place. She had had several abortions prior to her pregnancy with him; and the only reason she did not have another was that it appeared to be too dangerous to her health. It was into this hostile environment that Dan was born. Instead of expressing this hostility directly, the mother apparently felt so guilty about her feelings that she went overboard in the other direction, lavishing gifts upon him, giving him everything he asked, and solving any problems for him when his behavior got him into trouble. As a result Dan entered adult life immature in many ways and handicapped in his ability to assume responsibilities, since he had never been encouraged to assume any as he was growing up. So there are many ways in which children experience rejection, and all of us have had some taste of it. It is a matter of degree.

The human personality appears to be very sensitive

to feelings of rejection. This is particularly true for the child, for he has not learned to develop defenses for warding off such feelings and is relatively helpless to fight back in any way. It is inevitable that when the child feels rejected he will experience some emotional reaction to this rejection.

It should be emphasized here that it is difficult to describe an emotional experience in words, which are, of course, primarily intellectual. The young child has not developed the intellectual capacity to "think" in the terms we must use to describe an experience. Whatever processes the child uses, however, it seems undeniable that he experiences feelings of rejection and feelings of being loved at a very early age. As a matter of fact, it is likely that the child can sense how his parents feel about him before he can understand any of the words they say. Later, of course, the child encounters other experiences that are interpreted as rejection and that contribute to and reinforce these earlier feelings of rejection. The characteristic reaction of the child to these feelings is a growing sense of worthlessness.

## The Conspiracy of Silence

For example, the conspiracy of silence caused by parents' unwillingness and inability to talk openly with their children about sex can cause serious confusion and unnecessary damaging emotional experiences. The child, of course, concludes that the parents' reluctance to talk about such important feelings is the result of their mistrust and rejection. This is well illustrated by the following account by Rita, a young woman who was reared in a rough metropolitan area. She describes an incident that occurred when she was seven.

"It was the custom then to attend the local matinée

on Saturday. I sat, on a given Saturday, with a boy from down the street, and he said that if he were allowed to fuck me he would give me a dime. I had no idea what the word meant. I did know that it was forbidden to be used in school, and when other children used it on the playground it was always accompanied with more giggling and silliness than other profanity one heard at home or elsewhere. At any rate, all this incident consisted of was a kiss on the cheek and feeling of my underpants.

"That evening I went with my family to a birthday dinner at my grandmother's house. Midway through the meal I proudly asked, 'Guess what I did today?' When I made the announcement that I had 'fucked,' my father stood up in such a rage that his chair fell over. I can remember his words as plainly as if it had happened today: 'I am going to take this family home and teach them something.'

"We left immediately and I recall speeding through the city, over the streetcar tracks, racing a train to the crossing, and screeching to a stop in front of our house. When we got inside the house, I was spanked with the razor strap, which was the usual discipline for severe 'naughtiness,' and my mouth was washed out with soap. But I was never told the meaning of the word. As far as I knew it consisted of feeling a person's underpants or thighs."

So Rita was severely punished and condemned for what she had said, but she was given no explanation. She had no way of knowing that she had not "fucked" and must have been filled with much puzzlement, guilt, and embarrassment. This incident set the stage for another, which occurred five years later, when she was twelve. By this time Rita had moved, with her family, to a farm community. She speaks of what happened in the following way.

"My parents went to the city for a weekend toward the end of the school year. My sister and I stayed with a family who had three girls and two boys. One of the boys was also a sixth-grader. He was used to heavy work on the farm and, as I remember him, seemed more like sixteen than twelve.

"All of us slept that weekend in one large room, sort of a bunkhouse. During the night this boy came over to the bed where I was sleeping with his two sisters. He asked if he could get into bed with us, because he was cold. I recall awakening about dawn to discover he was feeling my breasts and thighs. I was very frightened and did not move a muscle. I do not know why I did not want him to know I was awake. Soon I heard his father outside the building calling for him to get up and help milk the cows.

"It was a school day and the family lived a sufficient distance from the road that his mother gave us a ride in a pickup truck to the bus stop. The boys rode in back, and I rode in the cab with his mother. Since I still was under the impression that what had happened that morning was called 'fucking,' I used that word as the appropriate one when I told the boy's mother, in fear instead of pride this time, what had taken place.

"She was a woman with no education, and at this point she became enraged and swore like a sailor. After she left me at the bus stop she took the boy home with her and questioned him. He denied even coming into bed with us.

"That evening, when my parents returned from the city, she told them what had happened. My parents then accused me of being resentful and jealous of the fact that my father had hired this boy to do some work and had apparently liked him. They never did ask me what had happened. I had begun to menstruate a month prior to this and, knowing nothing of the

mechanics of sex, was afraid I might have a baby.
When I asked my mother about this, she made it clear
she believed *nothing* had happened."

## Feelings of Worthlessness

When exposed to insensitivity such as Rita experienced
from her parents it is inevitable that a child would
feel rejected. And these feelings undermine whatever
feelings of value the child may have had and gradually
feelings of worthlessness develop. This process can be
diagramed as follows.

FEELINGS OF REJECTION

↓

FEELINGS OF WORTHLESSNESS

Perhaps the emotional logic of the child is something like this: "The most significant people in my life
—that is, my parents—do not appear to consider me to
be of personal worth, therefore I must be worthless."

As the child becomes older, he may or may not be
aware of feelings of worthlessness. Some people are
quite aware of such feelings. There is probably no
counselor who has spent time working with people
who has not had individuals say something like this:
"All of my life I have never felt I really mattered to
anyone. And I have always felt there must be something wrong with me."

There are others who have been somewhat successful in keeping their feelings of inadequacy and worthlessness out of their conscious thoughts by the means
of various kinds of psychological defenses, some of
which will be discussed later. But it is a universal experience. All of us have some of these feelings within
us.

## Feelings of Self-hate

When the child begins to have these feelings of worth-lessness as a result of feeling that he has been rejected, the next step in his emotional development seems to take the form of self-hate, as follows:

FEELINGS OF REJECTION

↓

FEELINGS OF WORTHLESSNESS

↓

SELF-HATE

Again we can imagine the emotional logic that takes place within the child. Probably it is something like this: "I seem to be worthless. I appear inferior to my parents and other people around me. I cannot respect myself, since they don't seem to respect me. Since I am worthless, I hate myself."

These feelings of self-hate may be maintained on a largely unconscious level. In fact there is every reason to think that the child would do everything possible to avoid bringing these feelings into awareness, no matter how strong they might be. To really hate oneself is a repelling, frightening idea, so much so that it is almost intolerable.

Perhaps the best example of extreme self-hatred that is at least partly conscious is the person in a suicidal depression. The self-hate is so strong and so intolerable that the only out for the person appears to him to be the murder of one's self, an act of extreme self-hate.

Because hate of one's self is so intolerable and is so threatening to the very roots of the person's being, most persons react with psychological defenses of one kind or another. We find some kind of "escape hatch" by which to avoid the full force of this terrible feeling that we are worthless and the object of our own hatred.

A strong case can be made for believing that it is this feeling of hatred toward one's self that lies at the root of most, if not all, personality difficulties and family problems that are not caused by a brain injury or some other physical malfunction. For the things that people do and say that result in their being described as having personality problems and that cause them difficulty in relationships with others can be seen as ways of escaping from self-hatred.

Before some of these ways of escape are examined in detail, it is well to note the principle that now comes in focus. As we shall see as we examine these escape hatches, each of them seems to have built into it the tendency to set up a negative reaction in other people that will lead to further feelings of rejection and therefore increase the individual's feelings of worthlessness and self-hate. This cyclical process might be illustrated as follows:

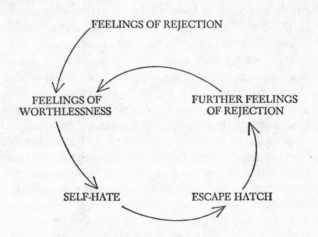

FEELINGS OF REJECTION

FEELINGS OF WORTHLESSNESS

FURTHER FEELINGS OF REJECTION

SELF-HATE

ESCAPE HATCH

Let us turn now to look at a specific example of how this process works.

## How Johnny Became a Bully

It was a rough day for Johnny, aged four, and his mother almost from the moment it started. Johnny was dawdling. He dawdled over getting dressed and he dawdled over breakfast. While his mother dashed around attempting to get Johnny's seven-year-old sister off to school, he made complaints about the food, which were not well received by his mother. Perhaps his mother's patience was shorter than usual because of the argument over finances that she and her husband, Bill, had had the night before. In any case, things went from bad to worse until mother informed Johnny that he would sit there and finish that food whether he liked it or not! And Johnny, with that innate desire to preserve his own individuality, did *sit* there for half an hour. Finally he ate enough of his food so that his mother, in total exasperation, decided the time had come to compromise and let him up from the table.

Shortly thereafter, Johnny went over to play with three-year-old Billy in the neighbor's backyard. His mother sighed with relief; now she would have some rest from what by then seemed like an endless involvement in unsatisfying family squabbles. The peace and quiet was short-lived. Soon there was a ring at the back door, and there stood Billy's mother, with Johnny in tow. Johnny, so the report went, had made an unprovoked attack on Billy; and if this was the sort of thing that was going to happen, Billy wasn't going to be allowed to play with Johnny any more. Johnny could not, or would not, give a coherent account of the attack and certainly could not be expected to realize that he had still been angry at his mother and had struck out at his playmate as a safer target.

Johnny's mother is confused and frightened at this point. Basically, she is frightened about her own anger. She feels it is wrong for her to be angry so much, and she feels discouraged and angry with herself when she becomes so upset with those she loves. Since she finds her own anger so intolerable, it is also difficult for her to accept the same kind of feelings in Johnny.

Billy's mother leaves, still obviously upset; Johnny's mother sits him down, tells him that he is bad, and asks what possessed him to do a terrible thing like that. Johnny feels she is rejecting him and that she doesn't understand him. And, of course, he doesn't understand himself and why he hit Billy. So Johnny feels rejected and begins to feel increasing feelings of worthlessness. What will he do now? He may try to escape from feelings of worthlessness and self-hatred by further bullying of Billy or some other playmate. Or perhaps he will switch to some other way of avoiding his feelings about himself. He might attempt to escape by becoming a show-off or braggart. Here, too, sooner or later, even though it may seem "cute" at first, people will tire of it, and he will feel further feelings of rejection. He has been caught in a cycle of rejection.

The question might be asked here, "Is not the person who is a bully or a braggart the one who loves himself or thinks too highly of himself, rather than the one who hates himself?" Further thought makes it clear, however, that if the child had genuine feelings of worth and value as a person, it would not be necessary for him to try to prove himself more powerful than others or better than others by bullying or bragging. He is attempting to escape from the nagging, haunting feeling that he is worthless by attempting to

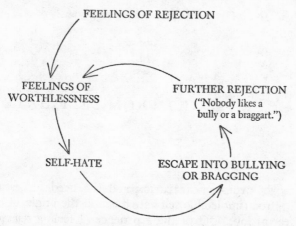

prove to others—and most of all to himself—that he is an individual of worth. Unfortunately, because of the way that other people react and because of his own feelings about the unsatisfactory ways in which he tries to prove his worth, he sinks more deeply into feelings of worthlessness.

Lest the picture appear too black, it should be emphasized that every child from time to time goes through experiences similar to Johnny's. It is not single isolated incidents that cripple personalities. When trends are established in relationships with parents, and when there is little to mitigate these trends, then serious problems can develop. It is important, however, to see that even minor incidents which cause feelings of rejection undermine to some degree a child's feelings of self-worth. We are again reminded that we are all caught in this human dilemma. It is not a question of whether we have feelings of worthlessness arising from feelings of rejection. The only question is, "How *much* self-hate do I have, and how much crippling effect does it have on my life?"

# III

# OUR FLIGHT FROM SELF-HATE

THE CYCLE OF REJECTION and the need for escape from intolerable self-hatred is also the origin of our fear of love. Out of the experience of feeling rejected, with subsequent feelings of worthlessness and self-hate, comes the child's feeling that love is risky. He probably never puts this feeling into words, even to himself, but the child's emotional logic must run something like this: "Since I hate my real self and know it to be worthless, I dare not be myself with others. If I am open and direct with people, they will see me as I am and hate me. If I love, I will only be hurt in return. I have had enough of that already, so I will find some other way of dealing with people."

The escape hatches not only provide a way of avoiding full awareness of self-hatred; they also help the person bypass the anticipated dangers of intimacy. And because he has feelings of worthlessness, the individual's desire to avoid the risks of love are increased because he lacks confidence in his ability to cope with emotional hurt when he experiences it.

When we look at other people's ways of dealing with their feelings of inadequacy it is often not too difficult to see that the escape hatches they use are ultimately self-defeating and lead to increased feelings of worthlessness and self-hate. But when we ourselves are caught in cycles of behavior that we have spent most of our lives developing it is not so easy to see our predicament or the desirability, much less the possibility, of breaking out of the cycle.

## Escape into Illness

As we turn to examine the major escape hatches, we see that some people escape from feelings of self-hate by developing *physical illnesses*. The research that has been done into psychosomatic illness makes it evident that the body operates as a total organism and that most physical illness can either be caused or greatly modified by emotional factors.

Two primary unconscious motivations appear to underlie such illness. In the first place, it seems evident that there is often a need to punish one's self. The person uses physical illness as an unconscious way of expressing his self-hate.

Another motivation seems to be that of asking for help. It is almost as if the person were saying to the world, "Won't somebody please take care of me?"

Therapists often report that they experience a great deal of trouble in dealing effectively with physical illness caused by emotional difficulties. This is probably because the individual, in being ill, usually does satisfy some of the needs that motivate the illness in the first place. He does succeed in punishing himself, and he often gains attention and care as a result of the illness. Both of these psychological gains, of course, are not ultimately satisfying, for there is usually growing resentment on the part of those who care for the ill person. This resentment is likely to be expressed in some form or other. Thus the stage is set for further feelings of rejection, more self-hate, and more pronounced physical problems.

Anne, a teen-age girl, did respond quickly to therapy, perhaps because her attacks of physical illness were not of long duration. She had for years had feelings of worthlessness and self-hate. Anne's relationship with her mother appears to have been particularly damaging. The mother demanded a great deal from Anne from the time she was a small child. By the time she was in junior high school she was doing most of the family's cooking, ironing, and housecleaning. But if her mother was ever pleased with her work, Anne never knew it. Instead she received a constant barrage of criticism from her mother, who demanded an impossible perfection. In addition, the mother saw to it that Anne had very limited contacts with other children her own age. As a result she became very shy.

When Anne was fifteen her problems became more acute following a frightening experience in which she was approached sexually by an older man, a man for whom she cared and who was important in her life. This experience was particularly frightening because the girl tended to accuse herself of acting in a seductive manner. She hated the thought that she might have had some part in encouraging the attempted sexual act. Shortly thereafter, during a period of time when she did not confide in anyone about this experience, she began to have an increasing number of what appeared to be migraine headaches. She also developed fainting spells for which there appeared to be no physical cause. On several occasions, at school, she lost consciousness and fell, without warning. Fortunately, when she was able to share the experience that she had been through with the counselor, was able to explore some of her feeling of unworthiness and self-hate and understand some of the sources of these feelings, the headaches and fainting spells soon ceased.

It is not difficult to see how this girl could have made illness a way of life, had she not secured help at the time she did. The cyclical nature of this type of illness can be observed in the following diagram.

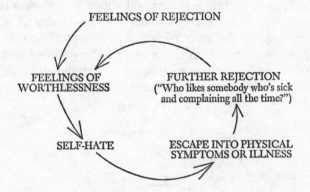

FEELINGS OF REJECTION

FEELINGS OF
WORTHLESSNESS

FURTHER REJECTION
("Who likes somebody who's sick
and complaining all the time?")

SELF-HATE

ESCAPE INTO PHYSICAL
SYMPTOMS OR ILLNESS

## Severe Mental Illness

When a person has been severely emotionally damaged as a child, the escape from self-hate may take the form of a *severe mental illness, or psychosis*. In this instance the feelings a person has about himself are so intolerable and life is so frightening that the person may escape into a fantasy world. He exchanges reality for unreality.

Perhaps the escape from self-hate is seen most clearly in instances where the person becomes someone else in his imagination, someone who is powerful, good, or important in some way. He may acquire an unshakable belief that he is Jesus, Napoleon, the Virgin Mary, Queen Elizabeth, or some other famous person. The immediate gain from the illness is obvious. The person is no longer the hated self who seemed worthless, hopeless, and a failure. Now he can look on himself as an individual of great importance and significance.

In spite of all our advances in the understanding and treatment of mental illness, however, the psychotic person is almost certain to experience further feelings of rejection. Society will almost surely deem it necessary to segregate him from "normal people," at least during the acute phases of the illness. When he does return to society, he is likely to be regarded with suspicion, prejudice, and fear, with little understanding or even tolerance of his emotional problems. Again the cycle can be diagramed.

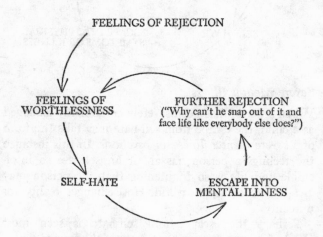

FEELINGS OF REJECTION

FEELINGS OF
WORTHLESSNESS

FURTHER REJECTION
("Why can't he snap out of it and
face life like everybody else does?")

SELF-HATE

ESCAPE INTO
MENTAL ILLNESS

## Addiction to Drugs and Alcohol

Alcoholism and other forms of addiction provide other ways of attempting to escape from feelings of self-hate. For a large majority of people the use of alcohol is a pleasant way to become more like the person they long to be. With the glowing warmth of two or three drinks, many people are able to talk more freely and enjoy their friends more openly. Usually too frightened of their love to reveal it, they are able to express their caring more openly and with more feeling.

The potential alcoholic, on the other hand, begins to rely on drinking as a way to avoid facing feelings of inadequacy, failure, and worthlessness. The alcohol numbs him to these feelings and, at least in the initial stages, helps him to escape his feeling of mediocrity and self-hate. He is less aware of his fear of suffering further rejection and so he mixes more with people, somewhat mitigating the terrible loneliness experienced in sober hours.

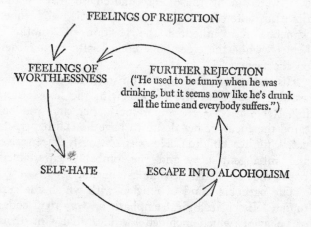

FEELINGS OF REJECTION

FEELINGS OF WORTHLESSNESS

FURTHER REJECTION
("He used to be funny when he was drinking, but it seems now like he's drunk all the time and everybody suffers.")

SELF-HATE

ESCAPE INTO ALCOHOLISM

But when he is sober again, feelings of self-hate come closer to the surface, fortified now by guilt feelings about the meaningless waste of his hours of drunkenness. The only answer to the resulting moodiness and sense of emptiness seems to lie in resorting again to drinking. Eventually the alcohol provides a more or less permanent "escape" from self-hate. Thus the alcoholic becomes more and more addicted. Meanwhile, he encounters ever more frequent rejection as one after another of his friends, and finally his family, find his drinking and his behavior while intoxicated increasingly unbearable and desert him. The only way of gaining relief from these further feelings of rejection, or so it seems to him, comes through further drinking. And so the cycle runs its course.

## Homosexuality

Homosexuality is another way of escaping feelings of self-hate. The story of Jim is somewhat typical. He was the last child in a large family. His sisters, however, were among the oldest children, so that by the time Jim entered school they were married and gone. Somehow Jim inherited the position of "mother's helper," while the older boys worked with their father on the farm.

His mother's influence on Jim went far beyond his washing the dishes and helping with the housecleaning. Religion was very important to her, and Jim became the focus of her desire to have her faith perpetuated in her children. He was obviously a sensitive and intelligent boy, and she probably entertained hopes that he would become a minister.

The particular kind of religion with which she surrounded Jim placed great emphasis on very rigid codes of behavior, which included the idea that Christians do not feel, let alone express, anger. This latter concept became very much a part of his life, and it widened the gulf between Jim and his father, who already seemed somewhat remote, for the father was a stern and blunt man who often displayed anger. Jim could hardly be expected to be his mother's kind of Christian and feel much kinship with his dad. Mother and "God" won the competition.

By the time he went away to college, Jim was apparently well established in his mother's way of life. But although it may not have been obvious, the danger potential was there. He felt uncomfortable in the rough-hewn coterie of men, as typified by his father. He had been cut off from both the skills and the emotions of that existence. Yet he also undoubtedly longed for some kind of place in a male world. With women he seemed, superficially at least, very much at ease. He shared many interests more typical of women in our culture. He was artistic and creative. Yet in relationships with girls that might have become intimate and meaningful at a deeper level, he tended to become guarded and aloof. It is evident that he had a profound underlying fear of being subtly manipulated and controlled by women, as his mother had done. All women were seen by him as threats to his individuality. It is not surprising that, when he was approached at college by men with similar problems, he fell quickly into homosexual practices.

Though he later married, he seemed unable either to give up his homosexuality completely or to achieve genuine intimacy with his wife, although they were able to have sexual intercourse. After several years of attempting to make a satisfying marriage, she finally left him.

With Jim, as with other homosexuals, his sexual relationships with men probably gave him some escape from his feelings of inability to satisfy his need for love and his feelings of worthlessness as a male. But his escape into homosexuality led to further rejection by parents, other relatives, friends, and acquaintances who proved typically intolerant of sexual problems. As so often is the case, even he and his homosexual partners tended to despise each other. Such rejection seemed to lead only to the search for the reassurance of new sexual partners in an unbroken cycle of rejection.

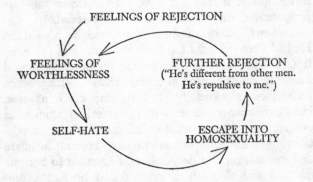

No attempt is being made here to explain fully why a person chooses one escape from self-hate rather than another, as, for example, why one person becomes an alcoholic and another becomes a braggart or develops symptoms of physical illness. There are many complex reasons for these differences. Some of them certainly have to do with the kind of rejection that is experienced. Chance occurrences may lead to the expression of one symptom rather than another. For example, it is possible that Jim, the homosexual just described, might have become an alcoholic if he had not been approached by an experienced homosexual and if his rigid religious training had not discouraged any experimentation with drinking. The purpose here, however, is to show that feelings of rejection, worthlessness, and self-hate lie at the root of these problems, whatever the various nuances may be.

There is also room for inborn differences within this general pattern. Perhaps, for example, it is possible that some people are chemically more susceptible to alcoholic addiction than others. This would not mean that alcoholism would be a certainty for such a person even if it were found that such potentials occur. Without the need to escape from severe feelings of inadequacy and self-hate, the individual would not likely become an alcoholic.

## Escaping Self-hate by Hating Others ✓

There are two escape hatches that it is well to examine in more detail because they play so important a part in many families. One of these is the attempt to escape from feelings of self-hate by *hating others*. This involves a mental process psychologists call <u>projection</u>.

When a motion picture projector casts a picture on a screen, what the viewer sees is not determined primarily by the screen, although its quality can affect the image. The picture comes from within the projector, although the viewer may become so "lost" in the drama unfolding on the screen that he is no longer consciously aware of the source of the image. In the phenomenon of projection, psychologically speaking, the individual is both the projection machine and the viewer. In other words, a person sees what he projects onto the screen.

In many ways, by using various scientific methods, psychologists have shown that all of us do a great deal of projecting, some of us more than others. In other words, when we look out at the world around us our view of reality is more or less distorted by the image we project, without conscious awareness, from our own minds. So, for example, psychologists have demonstrated that if we are shown a broken line drawing suggesting some image with which we are familiar, we have a tendency to complete that image in our mind when we look at the incomplete drawing.

Projection is an important consideration here, because we have a tendency to project onto others qualities or feelings that we cannot accept in ourselves.

Thus, for example, a woman who cannot accept her own sexual feelings may feel that every man who glances at her is out to seduce her.

Since the feeling that we hate ourselves is such a threat to us, we cannot accept it in ourselves. Projection of self-hate onto others becomes one readily available way of avoiding these feelings.

It is no surprise, then, that some children faced with frequent situations in which they feel rejected by others learn to avoid the feelings of worthlessness and self-hate by this means. Instead of being aware of the feeling "I hate myself," such a child will feel "*They* hate me!"

It is only a small step further, of course, for the child's reaction to be "Since they hate me, I hate them." The child then has a target toward which to express all of the hostility seething within him—hostility because he feels worthless and because he has been rejected.

When we project feelings we do not choose our targets indiscriminately. They usually make some kind of sense. A natural target for the child is the parents from whom he has felt rejection. And it is the child whose parents have been overly punishing and who have severely restricted the child's freedom who most often tends to develop the reaction "My parents hate me, therefore I hate them!"

When the child yells out his anger toward his parents or rebels against their directives, he is likely to meet more severe punishment and restriction. As a result, he feels more rejection and slips deeper into feelings of self-hate that is again converted into "You hate me, so I hate you!"

If this cycle is not broken, the hatred of others often widens in scope to people outside the family circle as the child grows older. Often those in positions of authority, who are probably unconsciously identified with the parents, become the target of increasing hatred; and so the child may get into difficulty with school officials and later with the police.

It was that way with Jerry. As a small child, Jerry came to feel that his parents cared more for his younger brother, Bob, than they did for him. There was a reason for this. Somehow Bob had early learned to comply with his parents' requests, so he was praised and seldom punished. Jerry, on the other hand, was not so compliant to their demands that he adhere to their rather strict requirements. He often disobeyed, and he was frequently punished by his parents, who meant well but knew no other way to cope with disobedience. Gradually, he learned not to rebel so openly, but his sullen acquiescence was often treated as rebellion. As a teen-ager he began to have more than his usual amount of trouble in school. He interpreted almost all efforts of schoolteachers to correct his work or make suggestions about his behavior as evidence that they, like his parents, were against him. More and more he began to dislike them and demonstrated his feelings by ditching school and causing disturbances in the classroom. The school authorities and teachers responded with punishments for his infractions, which Jerry interpreted as confirmation that they had it in for him.

Soon the police, too, became involved. Jerry began to be picked up for speeding and reckless driving almost as soon as he had a license. Now they, too, were enemies to be hated. It would be only a short step from there to thinking of all society as a part of the hated "others." Jerry apparently took that step, for a few months after his fourth traffic ticket he was apprehended and charged with a series of burglaries in his community. Perhaps the judge's sentence will harden him in his conviction that he is surrounded by enemies.

Thus the rebellion against parents who do not seem to care can spread to rebellion against a society that does not seem to care. And if a man like Jerry becomes a father, he will probably be too emotionally handicapped and frightened to express his love to his children. He, too, will probably be punitive and hurtful. And thus, unless the cycle is broken, the blight of self-hate perpetuates itself from one generation to another.

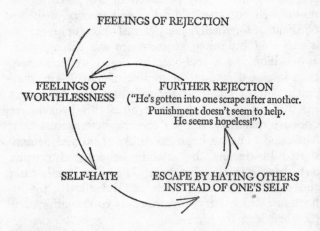

FEELINGS OF REJECTION

FEELINGS OF WORTHLESSNESS

FURTHER REJECTION
("He's gotten into one scrape after another. Punishment doesn't seem to help. He seems hopeless!")

SELF-HATE

ESCAPE BY HATING OTHERS INSTEAD OF ONE'S SELF

## Foredoomed Attempts to Please

Another escape hatch from feelings of hatred toward one's self is *the attempt to win acceptance from others by pleasing them*. It is important to examine this tendency closely because it is subtle and therefore often misunderstood. In the initial stages, at least, the children who are its victims are frequently mistaken as "healthy, well-adjusted children."

When they are caught in the bind of increasing feelings of worthlessness and self-hate, some children will, in their effort to escape, make desperate attempts to win acceptance by attempting to meet what they perceive to be the requirements of their parents. They attempt to please and thereby win their parents' love.

One might tend to assume that such a child would "come out all right." After all, one would think that the child, by attempting to please, would win expressions of love and acceptance and no cycle of rejection would result. Unfortunately, it usually does not work that way, for parents whose children take this approach to dealing with self-hate have probably created the child's feelings of rejection and worthlessness by making unrealistic demands on the child and by encouraging the child to feel that their acceptance of him is conditional upon his performance. It is as though the child feels the parents are saying to him, "We will love you if and when you live up to our standards."

Under these circumstances the child's efforts to win acceptance and a feeling of self-worth by attempting to please his parents are almost certain to fail for two reasons.

First of all, the child's performance will probably never be quite good enough. It is clear that the parents have considerable doubt about their own adequacy as parents and are afraid of the open expression of love, otherwise they would not have needed to make their love seem to hinge on the child's behavior. These same qualities will make it difficult for the parents to respond with real enthusiasm even to excellent accomplishments.

Betty, a teen-ager, apparently was attempting to win acceptance by pleasing. She was a student in a private girls' high school, where she attempted to become one of the "in" group by conforming to the requirements of the particular community of girls with whom she went to school. She dressed like them, spoke their jargon, and catered to the "in" leaders. Since she was a talented girl, she was fairly successful at this, and when time came for school elections she was elected secretary of the student body. She could hardly wait until the next weekend visit with her parents, because she was eager to tell them of her success. She walked into the house bubbling over with the exciting news. Her mother's only reaction was, "Why couldn't you have been elected president?" Since she was exposed to such attitudes of her parents all of her childhood, it is no wonder that now, fifteen years after that incident, she still tries to prove her worth to the world, her parents, and, most of all, to herself.

✝ The second reason why efforts to win acceptance through pleasing are doomed to failure is that the individual's self-hate is increased, because he feels a loss of freedom to be a genuine individual in his own right. When a child grows up with a feeling that he must strive at all times to perform adequately and that love will be given and withdrawn on the basis of his performance, he never feels free to be himself. He resents others and himself because he is not becoming an independent person who is loved and respected because he *is* rather than because of what he *does*.

The grading system in school lends itself to such predicaments for children. Nancy was reared in a strict, religious household in which great emphasis was put upon school success. She became so involved in the need to please by being successful in her schoolwork that she began cheating very early in her school life. Whenever a test was scheduled, she would suffer a great deal of anxiety about the possibility of not doing well. Whenever it was possible, Nancy would devise methods of cheating. On several occasions—when she saw no way of cheating successfully—she went to the playground swing during recess and deliberately twisted in it and twirled in such a way that she became physically ill. It would then be necessary for her to go home, thus avoiding the necessity of taking the test. She went through terrifying torments of guilt and self-hate, since she lived in a household where lying and cheating would be considered a great sin. Nancy felt that God condemned her. It is no surprise that she also believed no one could possibly love her for herself—and certainly could not love her as she had become—if they really knew her.

Yet on the surface Nancy managed somehow to appear to live a successful and happy life. She was able to conceal her self-torment from others. She appeared to win a good deal of acceptance, but all the time her self-loathing was being reinforced. It was not until she was in her forties and had a family of her own that she was able through psychotherapy to share these feelings. Only then could she experience relief from the feeling of being a fraud and discover that people's love for her was not based on the image of herself that she had so carefully constructed in order to win acceptance.

Nancy is an extreme example, to be sure, but there are many people who are caught in some form of the attempt to win acceptance through pleasing. Sometimes it is the "quiet one" in a classroom who never gives the teacher or anyone else any trouble, but who also never seems to be able to join in the fun in a spontaneous way and who is terribly afraid of making a mistake. Adults who have an obsession with keeping things organized or clean or who demand perfection of themselves in other ways likely developed the pattern trying to please parents. When these people became parents themselves they, too, because of their own fears and feelings of self-hate, may become subtly rejecting, giving the feeling to their children that they must perform at a certain standard if they are to win mother's or dad's love.

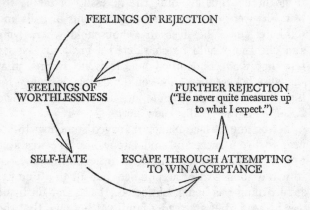

FEELINGS OF REJECTION

FEELINGS OF WORTHLESSNESS

FURTHER REJECTION ("He never quite measures up to what I expect.")

SELF-HATE

ESCAPE THROUGH ATTEMPTING TO WIN ACCEPTANCE

## When "Religion" Adds to the Problem

It is appropriate here to speak of the harmful effects that a certain kind of religious training can have on children's lives. Although they may speak of love as being of first importance in human affairs, churches often become preoccupied with rigid rules of conduct, betraying a deep mistrust of spontaneity in behavior. The church then tends to condemn any failure to measure up to its standards. Under these circumstances the church creates a community where the members do not experience a free-flowing experience of love for each other but rather one in which they feel on guard and constantly in danger of condemnation.

These attitudes, of course, extend into the family lives of members of the religious group. The result is that some "religious" families are among the most psychologically damaging to their children. Perhaps much of the damaging effect comes because of the confusing message that the judgments and the condemnation are a result of the love of the parents for the child. Such parents often say in effect, "We only say these things to you because we love you so much and want you to be happy." And the fact that the parents *are* sincere and do not recognize that their need to judge, condemn, and mistrust their children is the result of their own self-hate, mistrust of themselves, and resulting fears only makes the message that much more subtle and more difficult for the child to cope with.

Sheri is a young woman who grew up in this kind of a religious family. Her father was an attorney, and he was also a perfectionist and a staunch religionist. Sheri was always made aware that it was very important to him that she succeed in her schooling. In fact she felt his love was dependent on her achievement.

Although she was a very bright girl, Sheri did not respond favorably to these demands. She did not do well in school and dropped out of college, an action of which her father strongly disapproved. Not long thereafter, however, she—on her own initiative—became a skilled legal secretary as a result of her own initiative. She thoroughly enjoyed her work and made a good living for herself.

Instead of being delighted about her success, her father continued to express his disappointment and criticize her for not having made full use of her talents by securing a college degree. Whatever she did, it was never quite good enough.

It is not surprising that Sheri, having been exposed all her life in her "religious" home to such demands, has also tended to see God as demanding an impossible kind of perfection from her. She never thinks of God loving her just as she is. God is made into the image of her father.

It is not unusual at all in such circumstances that we come to imagine that God embodies the criticism we feel of ourselves and that which we feel from our "religious" parents. We become paranoid about God.

This feeling is illustrated by another woman who dreamed one night that Jesus was looking at her in a very stern and condemning manner. Gradually, in the dream, the face of Jesus changed into the face of her mother, who did indeed tend to be very critical of her, but subtly so and in the name of religion.

In families like this the force of religion and the religious community often feed into and become an important part of the cycle of rejection. The child initially feels rejection from parents who themselves are full of self-hate and fears and therefore are unable to express their love as openly as they might. As the child grows old enough to be impressed with somewhat more sophisticated ideas, religious teaching, formal and informal, may enter in to fortify these feelings of rejection. The subtlety of the teaching varies a great deal according to the orientation and the sophistication of the religious group. But the child is likely to receive the message that he is evil by nature and that he dare not trust his feelings or impulses. He is likely to feel, even though he may be assured that it is not true, that not only his parents but also God and the members of his religious community will not like him if he does not meet prescribed standards of behavior.

These are ideal conditions for the flourishing of feelings of worthlessness and self-hate, which are often accompanied by strong feelings of guilt, often of a generalized and unspecific nature.

Eventually the child seeks one or more ways of escape from the self-hatred in the form of some actual or fantasied, neurotic or delinquent behavior.

But there is no escape. If his feeling or behavior is detected, he feels condemned by parents and the religious community. If he is not found out, he is in the position—which may be even more psychologically dangerous—of feeling, "They'd sure condemn me if they really knew me." In either case he feels condemned by a critical "God" who sees all and knows his innermost thoughts. And so the cycle is completed as these further feelings of rejection intensify his feeling of worthlessness.

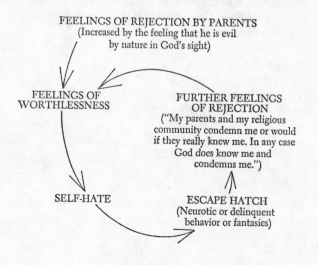

FEELINGS OF REJECTION BY PARENTS
(Increased by the feeling that he is evil
by nature in God's sight)

FEELINGS OF
WORTHLESSNESS

FURTHER FEELINGS
OF REJECTION
("My parents and my religious
community condemn me or would
if they really knew me. In any case
God *does* know me and
condemns me.")

SELF-HATE

ESCAPE HATCH
(Neurotic or delinquent
behavior or fantasies)

So our personality problems and difficulties with others have their origins in our childhood experiences. Our fear of love arises out of feelings of rejection and the subsequent feelings of worthlessness and self-hate that begin when we are children.

Because childhood experiences are recognized as being of crucial importance, the professions that offer psychological help are often accused, and perhaps with some justification, of teaching people to "blame their parents" for their problems. While there is no doubt that parents play an important role in child development, it is a waste of time to attempt to pin responsibility on them. It is much more helpful to see the problem in terms of the universality of the fear of love. As parents we are afraid of emotional closeness, even with our children. Perhaps this is not so surprising since no one matters more to us and, therefore, no one has greater power to hurt us. Consequently, we resist letting them see our genuine selves—how lonely, frightened, and capable of being hurt we are. Our children experience this withholding of ourselves and our genuine feelings as rejection.

IV

OUR FEAR OF FREEDOM

ONE OF OUR MOST deep-rooted ideals is our desire for
freedom, both at a personal and a collective level.
Words such as those from the New Testament—"You
will know the truth, and the truth will make you free,"
(John 8:32 R.S.V.)—strike a deeply emotional chord
in most of our hearts. Yet, while all of us pay lip service to freedom and our desire for it, we are also very
much afraid of it. We talk about personal freedom, but
we tend to shy from it.

Celeste was married to a man who had always
tended to be exceedingly critical of her. He made unreasonable demands of her and attempted to dominate
her entire life. She in turn tended to play a weak,
helpless role in relationship to him. In general, she
did little to oppose his bullying attitudes. When he
was around, at least, she was the obedient slave; and
he was the ruthless tyrant.

Things began to change, however, after Celeste
sought help through psychotherapy. Out of a growing
sense of her own value as a person she began to stand
on her own feet. She started doing things she did not
think he would tolerate. She refused to accept unjust
criticism. When he falsely accused her, she fought
back. To her amazement he did not react with the

brutality that she expected. Instead he showed that he felt more respect and warmth toward her than he ever had when she was so compliant. As her self-respect grew, his respect for her also appeared to grow. Gradually, she became aware of the exhilarating fact that she was not enslaved. She was much more free to do as she wished than she ever thought she could be.

But at this point Celeste had a very interesting reaction. When she spoke of it, she said, "You know, I have the funniest feeling. Now that I have this freedom to do everything I've ever wanted to do, I don't know what to do with it. I guess I'm frightened. It's almost as though I needed him to criticize me, and push me around, and make me feel trapped!"

The conclusion that we are afraid of freedom seems inescapable when we examine the lengths to which we go to enslave ourselves. For example, men and women who see a therapist for help with personal or family problems often spend much time trying to convince their counselor and themselves that they are not free to do what they want to do. Listen to what some of them say, and you will probably recognize some of your own feelings.

A mother says, "I can't do the things I'd really like to do. I feel it's my duty to spend my free time with my youngsters."

A husband says, "If I were ever really myself and told my wife how I really feel about her, she'd leave me in a minute."

Nearly everyone says, "If I said the things I really want to say to people, no one would like me." Or, "I can't let people see what I'm like because then they wouldn't have anything to do with me."

And everyone says, "I have so many things I just *have* to do, that I'm never free to do the things I *want* to do."

A working wife says, "I'd like to quit my job, but I don't see how we could get along."

A nonworking wife (an unemployed wife, that is!) says, "I really want to work, but I feel it's my duty to stay at home."

*t*    Perhaps it can be summed up by stating that we all have a tendency to say in one way or another, "Poor me, I'm just a helpless victim of circumstances."

My, how we kid ourselves! For when we are realistic about it, we have to recognize that there are few if any things that we *have* to do. We do what we do and avoid doing what we do not do because we choose it that way. We always have alternatives.

So it is with the "trapped" feeling in marriage. One man said to his wife, "If it weren't for you and the kids, I'd go to the beach and become a surfer."

He was considerably shook up when his wife replied, "Well, if that's what you want, why don't you go ahead. Nothing's really preventing you!"

Later, in telling about it, he said, "You know, she was right! If I really wanted to, I could leave her and head for the beach. But when I no longer felt trapped, I realized I don't really want to be a beach bum. In fact the whole idea is rather distasteful!"

As long as he could maintain the fantasy that he was trapped, this man could ignore the frightening fact that he loves his wife and children and is staying married by choice rather than because he must.

The old cliché is true. We don't *have* to do anything but die and pay taxes. (And, of course, we can refuse to do the latter if we are willing to suffer the consequences!) We always have alternative courses of action, but we constantly try to convince ourselves otherwise. We must be terribly frightened of discovering that we are free to do pretty much what we want to do.

## Our Fear of Change

Our fear of freedom expresses itself in many ways. *Our resistance to change* is probably one such expression. For example, during the times recorded in the New Testament early Christians apparently found it very difficult to give up the old ceremonial laws that had been traditional with Judaism for centuries. One would think that this would have been easy for Christians to do. They had embraced a young faith that said it was no longer necessary to perform the many daily ritualistic laws that virtually enslaved those who seriously tried to follow them. The reluctance to give up such observances seems hard to understand unless we see that it must have been terribly frightening to people suddenly to have almost unlimited freedom.

And no doubt the same sort of thing happens constantly today in both our institutional and our personal lives. In our religious, political, educational, economic, and social life, we probably cling to many time-consuming rituals and customs that no longer have any relevance to life. They probably serve mainly to keep our daily lives somewhat predictable and provide the security of a self-limited freedom.

Much of the tension between generations likely results from the resistance to change that parents express. Most changes, like the more extensive use of the automobile, for example, seem to us parents to be in the direction of granting our children more freedom. We are frightened of freedom for ourselves; we are also afraid of our children having it.

## Those Troublesome "Shoulds and Should Not's"

Fear of freedom also expresses itself in various *legalistic approaches to life*. We have a great propensity for regulating life in minute detail and insofar as possible deciding in advance what is right and what is wrong or what is socially acceptable or unacceptable.

And if we are successful in doing this, usually with the aid of a religious group or social class, then we can know in almost every situation what we "should" do. Then we no longer have to think or feel. We can rather automatically do what we "know is right"; or, failing that, we suffer the "appropriate guilt" for the "sin" or "social blunder" that we have committed. This makes for a safe, regulated kind of life. But it also tends to be a joyless life from which most of the spontaneity and creativity has been removed.

Although it is often maintained that a sense of responsibility demands a clear-cut view of right and wrong, it is more likely that such legalistic approaches actually undermine personal responsibility. For shades of gray always exist in ethical situations. And when we ignore these shades of gray, arbitrarily seeing all factors as black or white, we take ourselves off the hook of wrestling with the subtleties of the situation. We are in a position where we can "uphold the right" and "denounce the evil."

## The Overorganized Life

Another very common way of keeping tight reins on freedom is by *overplanning and overorganizing life.* Many a housewife, for example, finds it difficult—if not almost impossible—to "drop everything" on a "moment's notice" and go on a picnic with the family. Perhaps there are dirty dishes in the sink or disarray in the house and she is certain she couldn't relax and enjoy herself if she left these jobs undone. And there is every likelihood that she might not, for many find it difficult to enjoy the spontaneity that can enrich life. The freedom appears to be too frightening.

It will come as no surprise to some to hear that family vacations are sometimes unhappy occasions despite the high hopes entertained when the family started out, car loaded down, for distant destinations. One couple who had experienced such disappointments made another attempt after some months in psychotherapy. The therapist was delighted when he received a picture postcard from Canada with a very brief message: "Having wonderful time! Why?"

Well, why not? Likely there are a couple of reasons why we often manage to be miserable on vacations. For one thing the family is together—let that read TOGETHER—more than at any other time, and that physical closeness that creates the possibility of emotional closeness is probably frightening to us, with the result that every member of the family, in a concerted effort to eliminate this frightening possibility, manages in one way or another to get on the nerves of everyone else.

The other reason is that we are confronted with all that freedom. We have two weeks in which we can do as we please and go where we please. No alarm clocks jangling, no school bells telling us to move from one class to another, no time clocks to punch, no precise hour when dinner must be on the table, no projects to be completed by such-and-such time. We are free, and it scares us!

So how do we meet this "crisis" in freedom? Many of us meet it with a frenzy of planning. We go to the drawer, pull out our maps, and make an itinerary. "Now let's see, we'll sleep here the first night, then go over there, eat lunch in this town, spend an hour on this beach, and drive on to that place before dark, and

. . . and, oh yes, we'd better call the automobile club and have them make all the reservations along the way for us so there won't be any hitches in THE PLAN." See how hard we work sometimes to take away all that frightening freedom?

Planning, organization, and reducing some routine tasks in life to habit can perform the useful function of permitting the individual to live a freer and more creative life. If, for example, a housewife can sit down and plan a week's menus for the family so that she can do her shopping in one trip, a lot of time will be saved and needless last-minute worry eliminated about "What in the world are we going to eat tonight?" She has gained some free time by her planning. If she becomes a slave to her menus, however, it is quite another story. If she is no longer free to change her mind for a personal or family whim, she has sacrificed one of the pleasures of spontaneous living. Her rigidity becomes her defense against freedom, which frightens her.

Every home and almost every work situation provides countless opportunities to overplan and overorganize our lives. Many a businessman has spent his life "tending to details" without ever asking himself how relevant and how necessary the details are. The freedom to see creative ways of changing his routines and expanding his productivity with all of the necessary risks involved may have been too frightening.

### Rituals and Compulsions

Our fear of freedom also expresses itself in other ritualistic and compulsive behavior. So, for example, when a person—like Lady Macbeth—has a compulsion to wash his hands many times a day, the behavior not only provides a symbolic way of dealing with guilt feelings, but it also gives the person something with which to be preoccupied. It is almost as though he has unconsciously concluded that "idle minds [and hands] are the devil's workshop" and has substituted a meaningless activity to keep both busy.

All of us probably do some of this sort of thing in one way or another, if it is only in making a "game" of stepping on every crack (or avoiding stepping on any cracks) in the sidewalk. Some executives become busier and busier, having to work longer and longer hours. Although they may not be consciously aware of it, they may be doing this because they feel much more comfortable and safe at work than they do in their "free" time when they could be with their families or engaged in other exciting, but frightening, activities.

Extreme emphasis on cleanliness and its preservation often performs similar functions. One young woman described how her mother had set aside the "living" (!) room of the house so that no member of the family entered it except on Christmas and Easter. Although there was no physical barrier to the room, even the family dog avoided it, because he somehow got the message that to enter it was to invite disaster. "As a matter of fact," she said, "the cleaning lady was a very important part of our household because *she* got to go in there every week!" One wonders how the parents feel about their perfectly preserved "living" room with its unmarred furniture now that the children are married and gone. It certainly represents some lost opportunities in living. But living is frightening.

*Other Fears*

Sometimes fear of freedom is expressed in *other specific fears that limit our freedom*. Many such fears have been catalogued and given "phobia" names. There is fear of open places, closed places, high places, crowds, snakes, spiders, heart attack, death, being alone, and so forth. All of us experience some of these fears. They may be very mild or very intense. There may be considerable grounds for them in reality, or they may be quite unrealistic.

Much can probably be said about the symbolic meaning and origin of these fears in our lives, but their function appears to be that of limiting our freedom. Any one of these fears, if taken seriously, can limit our activities. And even if we attempt to ignore them and act in spite of them, they are likely to enter our minds and keep us from enjoying our freedom.

A young married woman tells how she becomes very uneasy whenever she goes a few miles from home. And she remains anxious until she returns. It is easy to see how she might live out her life in a "geographical box" if she does not find relief from this fear. She might well deprive herself of a whole world of adventure.

A young executive was bothered daily by the fear that his children would die. Every morning, before leaving on the long commuting trip to his office, he would have to go into each child's room and check to make sure each was breathing. During the working day the fear would frequently recur and he would call home to "check up on things." To go out of town on a business trip of several days would be almost intolerable.

Thus he kept himself in bondage. He was too preoccupied with his fear to relax with his children or fully express his love for them or allow himself the freedom to "enjoy them while he had them." Fatherhood was more frightening than it was fun.

## Demands and Obligations

We also express our fear of freedom by *seeing much of our lives in terms of demands and obligations.* Few of us can claim we lack talent, for whatever shortage of abilities we may have, most of us have a real knack for playing this game!

It is Saturday afternoon and the wife says, "Harry, how about watching the kids for the rest of the afternoon while I go shopping?" Now, Harry may not feel at all enthusiastic about this plan for his afternoon. But there is a good chance that he will feel some obligation ("After all, she does work pretty hard, too!") and will agree (by a grunt) with the proposal. But he may also feel that she has made an unreasonable demand. So he makes a few grumbling "bitches" about it, and the wife goes off feeling hurt, angry, or guilty, with some of the fun taken out of her expedition.

By playing the demand-obligation game Harry has blinded himself to the alternatives that he had. What are some of the things he might have said? "Honey, I was just going to call a couple of the guys and get together with them. How about calling a baby-sitter?" Or, "Gee, I was looking forward to spending the afternoon with you and the kids. Is there any other time you could do it?" Or, "I was planning to do some things around the house that I can't do if I have to watch the kids. Please call in a sitter."

Of course, there is always the chance, and perhaps not so remote either, that if Harry were aware of his alternatives and felt free to exercise them, he might genuinely enjoy playing with the children for the afternoon. But with the help of the demand-obligation game he manages to keep himself miserable and "unfree."

If you think *you* don't play this game, look at your gift-giving habits. See how often you tell yourself that a gift is expected or that you "owe" it to a person, thereby blunting your enjoyment in giving as an expression of your love.

One of the tricky aspects of the demand-obligation game is that, when we rebel against what others expect of us and against our own feelings of obligation, we are no more free than when we accede to them. If Harry flatly refuses to stay home with the children *because* it is expected of him, he has not really acted freely on the basic question of whether he would enjoy that time with his youngsters.

Probably many beatnik types are so busy rebelling against society's expectations that they are not free to ask themselves whether they are living the life most satisfying to themselves. Whenever we perceive life primarily in terms of others' expectations, we are less than fully free.

*Not being ourselves with others* is another way we often express our fear of freedom. None of us is completely ourselves all of the time in our encounter with others, and no doubt some lack of candor is often necessary, even desirable, in our complicated society.

But we overwork it, for we constantly tell ourselves in all kinds of situations that we cannot really be ourselves. We say that we can't be genuine with another because: "He's not really capable of understanding how I feel." Or: "He wouldn't love me any more." Or: "She's too old [or too young] to understand what I'm talking about." Or: "He hasn't read as much about these psychological things as I have, and it would be completely over his head if I told him how I feel." Or:

"He has so many troubles at the office I don't want to burden him with my feelings about what goes on here at home." Or: "She reacts emotionally whenever I say how I feel, so I've just learned to keep my mouth shut."

So we find various plausible "reasons" for not being ourselves with people. But it is likely that the real reason is that the freedom to be ourselves is frightening to us.

Many other things some of us do could be interpreted as expressions of our fear of freedom. *Some people live vicariously,* substituting imaginary lives for the adventure of living: "I guess I read an average of six or seven mystery novels a week."

*Psychosomatic illnesses* probably perform this, among other, services: "I'm sorry, but I have another one of my sick headaches tonight and just can't go out."

*Intellectualism* provides a way of substituting rumination for spontaneous living: "Doctor, I've read just about every psychology book I can get my hands on. I can't understand why I keep on having troubles."

## Mistrusting Ourselves

With all the ways people have of expressing their fear of freedom it may be fair to say that the most unlimited ability that the human animal has is that of building cages around itself. And once we build our cages we work hard to keep them in constant repair.

What is so frightening about freedom? We cherish it. We fight for it. Yet we run from it and go to great lengths to avoid an awareness of it. Why?

One reason we are afraid of freedom is that *we do not trust ourselves.* We are afraid of what we would do if we were not restricted in some way.

One woman described a lifelong fear of high places. When she began to explore her feelings further, she became aware that she had always been afraid that if the opportunity presented itself she might jump to her death. By being afraid of and avoiding such places she was able to bypass the risk that her mistrust of herself told her was involved.

Another young wife and mother suffers considerable inconvenience because she has never learned to drive. As she talked about it, it became clear that the freedom to come and go as she pleases is too frightening. "I'm afraid of what I might do," she said. "I might start running around and begin neglecting my home and family." And so she keeps herself immobile and as dependent on her husband as possible.

All of us, no doubt, have some kind of fear like this. We are afraid that if we ever "let ourselves go" we would be likely to "run wild" or become alcoholics, or rapists, or "lazy, no-good bums," or neglecting parents.

It follows, of course, that our distrust of ourselves is rooted in our self-hate. It is as though we were constantly warning ourselves to be on guard against ourselves: "Look out, now, this guy is no damn good. Let him out of your sight and he's liable to do most anything. Keep him hobbled. And don't let down your guard for a moment."

In reality, however, it is not the genuinely free person who "runs wild," becomes an alcoholic, or lacks the motivation to be productive. On the contrary, behavior that is destructive to the self or to others is an indication that the person is enslaved to repressed feelings that drive him and that he cannot face openly. Such behavior is the by-product of self-hate.

Perhaps there is some justification for our mistrust

of freedom if we have lived our lives denying freedom to ourselves. Just as a bird who has spent all its life in a cage might be bewildered if released and not know how to handle "life in the wild," so we, too, may not be very well prepared to handle freedom. Many people need professional help as they seek to grant themselves greater personal freedom.

A second reason we are afraid of freedom is that *freedom, like love, means vulnerability*. When we are free and spontaneous in our relationships with others, our guard is down. We are open to the possibility of being hurt. Consequently, we often keep ourselves "tied up" emotionally.

Couples often have the mystifying and frustrating experience of discovering shortly after marriage that they no longer have such a strong, delicious desire for each other as they had before. Sometimes they immediately conclude that they no longer love each other.

This is probably incorrect, for love is not so unstable a quality as all that. What has happened is that the couple has become frightened, since marriage is so intense a relationship with so much potential for being hurt. They react to their fear by unconsciously cutting off their freedom to experience and express their love. And, of course, they "discover" all kinds of misleading and irrelevant reasons for their change of feelings.

Sometimes we pick safe moments to be free. One wife complained that the only time her husband was affectionate was invariably when he was about to leave for work. At that moment he would become the loving, cuddly husband of whom she had dreamed. At practically all other times he would be cool and aloof.

It appears evident that he felt free to be loving at that moment when he "just had to leave" within five minutes. For then it was relatively safe for his love to come out of hiding. It could not possibly lead to anything further, which might mean more vulnerability. He could hug her and run!

So our fear of freedom does make some kind of sense, emotionally. We feel we can't be trusted with freedom and to be free is to risk being hurt.

But understanding why we fear freedom does not make it any less desirable as a goal in life. For in actuality our enslavement to fear is more hurtful to us than freedom. Avoidance of freedom exacts a heavy toll in our lives.

## Prices We Pay

For one thing, *our fear of freedom results in inner tension*. We have a virtually irrepressible desire to be more spontaneous and free. Since this desire is frightening, a conflict situation is present. We have to expend great amounts of energy keeping our cages in constant repair.

Energy thus expended in maintaining rigid control of ourselves puts a strain on us physically and emotionally. No doubt many physical and emotional problems are associated with this strain.

Our *fear of freedom also frequently leads to numbness of one's self*. When we do not feel free to be ourselves, one way out is gradually to cut ourselves off from awareness of our feelings.

Extreme instances of this occur in certain schizophrenic patients who seem totally incapable of experiencing a genuine emotion of any kind. Life and the freedom to feel have become so frightening that they have retreated into a world where there is no feeling.

But deadness to the self is not limited to such individuals. All of us in some degree have retreated from complete awareness. And to this extent we have deprived ourselves of the opportunity of living life at its fullest. Often this numbness affects our relations with others, and we find it difficult to sense how we really feel toward others.

Apparently, even the most basic senses can become somewhat dulled, giving all of life a kind of gray bleakness. And it is not unusual for a person who has been making progress in psychotherapy to report a new sense of awareness. The grass may seem greener. Natural beauty, unnoticed before, is seen with "new" eyes; and there is a fresh feeling of aliveness in one's body.

3 · *Fear of freedom also often cuts us off from the experience of love*. When we are not free to be ourselves, we are staying at a distance from others. Since we do not let others see us as we are and since we withhold our true feelings from them, we make it almost impossible for them and ourselves to feel emotionally close. And if the other person, in spite of our masks, appears to care for us, we always have an out. We can say, "He doesn't love me for what I am. I've seduced him into caring for me, and he likes me only because of what I let him see of me. If he really knew me, he would no longer care for me."

Thus we persuade ourselves that we dare not give up our slavery to our masks. And at the same time we also protect ourselves from making the frightening discovery that those who love us, love us in spite of— not because of—the masks we wear. In this way we perpetuate our fear of spontaneity.

Our fear of freedom is especially evident in two particular areas that deserve individual examination. We are afraid of the freedom to be angry and of the freedom to be aware of and enjoy our sexual feelings.

# V

## OUR FEAR OF ANGER

AN AMERICAN PROTESTANT CHURCH is having its annual business meeting. Reports of the various
church organizations read in monotonous tones suggest that the meeting is occurring more because someone feels it necessary rather than because of any vital
interest. Sparks of life appear briefly. A momentary
flurry arises over whether the women's donation from
the proceeds of their annual bazaar should be sent to
foreign missions or put in the fund for a new carpet in
the sanctuary. But this sporadic flash hardly ruffles the
surface as the meeting drones on drearily.

Finally the last report ends; the congregation stirs
restlessly. The moderator now also appears anxious to
be done. He asks routinely if there is other business
as he gathers up his papers. He looks up, surprised,
when a man at the back of the room stands up. The
room rustles with curiosity as the man steps to the
aisle and makes his way forward. Something about
him commands attention. It is not the way he is
dressed. His clothes are average enough—clean and
neat, but with a careless air, as though he did not give
much thought to them. It is more the man himself.
His determined stride speaks of strength. His face is
somewhat flushed. The room is quiet by the time he

reaches the front and turns around. Then he begins to speak:

"I'm sick and tired of this church—and you people! You're miserable frauds and hypocrites! You talk fine words about loving one another, then you cut each other to pieces behind each other's backs. You don't even have the courage to let people know to their faces how you really feel about them. It's disgusting! What miserable frauds you are! Oh, you have a beautiful building here. And you are fine-looking and well-dressed people, but your church is dead inside, and you are dead inside, full of rottenness and pretense! You 'fine Christians' are just about as low as you can get!"

Can you imagine the shock and surprise of a congregation if such an event really happened? At the very least it would be safe to say that no one in the room would any longer be bored! Most of those present would probably be critical. Some might say, "Well, there may be some truth in what he's saying. But why does he have to get so worked up about it? That's not going to accomplish anything!"

Above all else there would probably be a reaction of fear on the part of the audience. The intensity of the man's anger would be frightening, for we are not used to hearing such feelings so clearly expressed, particularly in this setting. And there would be fear about what it would mean to the church, fear that the congregation would be split asunder by the angry blast and the reaction that would follow. And for those who would disagree with the man and feel their anger mount within themselves, there would be fear of their own feelings and how they might express them. For we have learned to be afraid of our anger.

## Not Always Meek and Mild!

Yet it is an interesting, though usually ignored, fact that the founder of the Christian faith is portrayed in the New Testament as having become as angry with the religious leaders of his day as was this fictional character. And Jesus expressed his anger just as openly and as vehemently. The anger rings through unmistakably, especially when it is translated into the modern vernacular, as Phillips has done. Here are some of the phrases from the twenty-third chapter of the Gospel of Matthew that are attributed to Jesus:

"Alas for you, you scribes and Pharisees, play actors. . . . You blind leaders . . . you blind fools . . . you utter frauds . . . what miserable frauds you are . . . whitewashed tombs, which look fine on the outside but inside are full of deadmen's bones and all kinds of rottenness. . . . You are a mass of pretense and wickedness. . . . You serpents, you viper's brood, how do you think you are going to avoid being condemned to the rubbish heap. . . . On your hands is all the innocent blood spilled on this earth. . . ." (Phillips)

It is not surprising that the church has tended to ignore the angry Jesus in its use of him as an example of a mature and creative person. For the Christian church, most other religious groups, and our culture in general have been mistrustful of feelings of anger and frightened of any spirit of freedom that would encourage its direct expression.

## We Condemn Anger

The message comes to us in many ways and from many sources. We are encouraged to feel "guilty of wrongdoing," or "immature," or "temperamental and unstable" when we are aware of feelings of anger, especially when we "give in" to these emotions and express them.

Listen to some of the ways we persuade ourselves to avoid anger in various relationships.

"Parents, never become angry with your children. Their personalities will be warped, and they'll feel rejected. Above all, don't punish them while you're angry. If you have to punish them, do it in cold blood!"

"Children, never get angry with your folks. You must respect them and to be angry is to be disrespectful. Furthermore, they won't love you if you're angry at them."

"Husbands and wives, don't get mad at each other. A happy marriage comes only when you ignore the things that irritate you and choke down any anger you feel. And above all, never let the children hear you in any kind of disagreement."

"Bosses, don't tolerate anger from your employees. They'll never respect you if you allow them to get away with any expression of anger."

"Employees, never let the boss see you're angry at him. Swallow your anger. You may get ulcers, but you'll keep your job longer!"

You see how we handle this business of anger? We say it is wrong to feel angry and dangerous to our relationships to express it. Thus we have made the suppression of anger in our society an ideal. This attitude is expressed in a letter written to the editor of a magazine in which an article by the author of this book, "The Creative Use of Anger," appeared. The correspondent wrote:

. . . Perhaps I am psychologically abnormal, I don't know. But this I do know, that if, like the husband mentioned, I had scolded my wife so angrily as to hurt her and make her cry, I should feel that I had definitely sinned and ought to seek forgiveness both from her and from God; and the shame at my behavior would have stayed with me a long time.

*Self-expression* is a popular word, but somewhat indefinite. One speaks of his "better self," implying the existence of some other less good. Which one ought we to express? I, for one, feel that whenever an unworthy emotion (and I include here anger toward one's nearest and dearest) is expressed in action, a person is really degrading himself. . . .*

This is an excellent statement of the attitude that would be expected to develop from the explicit and implicit teachings of most representatives of the Christian church.

And a similar attitude tends to be adopted by most of us whether we are religiously oriented or not. One man was describing how he avoided expressing any anger or irritation toward his wife. When he was asked if he were afraid of his anger, his reply was immediate, "Of course I am. Everybody should be. When I'm angry I say things I don't mean. And that's not good."

And often we frown at or laugh at (which may be much worse) those who become concerned enough over matters to express anger. Often, for example, in public hearings on community issues the person who becomes emotionally involved enough to speak heatedly about an issue is subject to ridicule; and his ideas are frequently discounted because they are expressed angrily. The implication is made that the person "got carried away" with his emotions. Therefore, what he said must not have made sense. Yet in fact we often speak most lucidly in the heat of emotion. Somehow

* *Presbyterian Life,* Oct. 15, 1964.

we have assumed a sort of pseudoscientific attitude by which we fulfill our need to suppress anger. We have concluded that when ideas are presented "logically," "rationally," and without emotion they must be objective and therefore nearer the truth than ideas about which we become excited and emotional.

## How We Learn to Suppress Anger

*How do we learn to mistrust our anger and pass this mistrust on from one generation to another?* After all, the idea that anger has a legitimate and inevitable place in life has been stated many times before. Yet the suppression of anger remains an actual, though sometimes disavowed, ideal for most of us.

Our mistrust of our anger is learned, of course. And we learn it because it is taught to us. And the teaching begins early. Even small babies are frequently punished for "angry" behavior and rewarded for behavior that is more pleasing to the parents. As the child grows older, the training becomes more specific and explicit. The child is told not to express anger toward parents, or brothers and sisters, or others. He is taught that anger is bad and that it is bad because it is the opposite of love.

Most parents are too sophisticated these days to say, "If you get angry with me, it means you don't love me." Or: "If you get mad at me, I won't love you any more." Or: "If you do something, and I get angry with you, it means I don't love you." But despite our intellectual sophistication about these matters, we still often give our children exactly these messages. And we give them because we are not so sure that they are not true.

This is probably the most important way in which the ideal of the suppression of anger is maintained in our culture. A perpetual cycle is set up. We, as parents, having been subtly indoctrinated as children, cannot accept within ourselves the anger that we all experience. Our inclination is to avoid admitting our anger and dealing directly with our guilt about it. It is much easier for us to recognize and condemn the anger we see in our children.

So when our children express anger toward us, we react quickly to their "talking back" or "smarting off." The anger *we* express under these circumstances is, of course, "justified" because we are doing it "for the good of the child" and to "teach him a lesson." In other words, we have been "righteously indignant."

Our children, then, through many of these experiences, come to feel guilty about their anger when they feel it and more so when they express it. In order to please us and society they may try to suppress entirely this "evil" side of their nature. Unless the continuing cycle is interrupted, they, too, will eventually become parents well prepared to teach their children to mistrust their feelings of anger.

Another reason we learn to mistrust our anger is that we often have little opportunity to learn as children that we can be very angry without being dangerous. Often the only message the child hears is that if he becomes angry the outcome is likely to be disastrous. He is apt, for example, to understand that if he becomes angry with the boy next door he is liable to club the boy over the head with a baseball bat or be in danger of being clubbed. Under these circumstances he has little opportunity to learn that he can express anger directly and openly without the necessity of resorting to harmful violence.

One frightening reality is that there is indeed danger when a person has been encouraged to view himself along these extreme lines, so that he says of himself, "If I don't keep my anger suppressed, I'm likely to hurt someone." When the emotional overload of anger eventually piles up beyond the point where it can be suppressed, such a person is not prepared to act any way but violently, with the flood of backed-up emotion suddenly released.

Children also learn to mistrust their feelings of anger because their parents make it apparent that they are afraid of their own anger. Some parents go to great lengths to avoid letting the children see them fight. They feel so frightened and guilty about their anger that they assume it would be very frightening and emotionally damaging to their children for them to witness their parents in a heated argument.

What the children often witness are sullen silences between their parents that are probably frightening to the child because he has no idea what they are about and yet senses the anger. The child often interprets these silences as much more serious breaches between the parents than they actually are. And when the child does happen to overhear a fight between the parents (perhaps without their knowledge), it may seem as though the family is disintegrating, since he has been taught by word and implication that anger is a cataclysmic and catastrophic occurrence in human relationships.

But even if the parents were successful in hiding all their disagreements, the results would probably still be harmful; for the child would be likely to feel even more guilty and frightened about his own anger when he has no opportunity to observe similar feelings in his parents' dealings with each other.

On the other hand, when parents make little or no attempt to hide their anger from their children, but have not learned to fight creatively, it is certain to be frightening to the children. Such fights lead nowhere. Perhaps when the argument begins, dad stomps out of the house or mother withdraws behind a bitter wall of silence. Or perhaps the fighting degenerates into an incessant bickering back and forth that fails to clarify the real issues.

The fears that keep the parents from dealing creatively with their anger are almost certain to infect the child under such circumstances. For the child has been denied the opportunity to see those he loves dealing openly and realistically with anger. He has not been able to witness his parents in a natural ebb and flow of anger openly and directly expressed, resulting in relief of tension, clearing of the air, and the good feeling of having been oneself, followed by the reassertion of their deep affection also being expressed openly and directly.

## Our Self-destructive Use of Anger

When we suppress anger, insofar as its direct expression is concerned, we inevitably pay some price for this denial of ourselves. As a matter of fact, the idea of suppression of anger involves some self-deceit, for we always "express" our anger in some way. Attempting to suppress anger is like trying to push an inflated inner tube under water. When we manage to push one side of it under, it pops out at some other point. So when we suppress the direct expression of anger it manifests itself in some indirect way. We may take it out on ourselves or on others. Usually our reactions involve some form of both.

There is an emotional logic in our tendency to turn our anger inward in some self-damaging expression. After all, as we have seen, we have been taught to hate and mistrust this part of ourselves. We have been taught that anger is condemnable, so when we feel angry our feelings of self-hate are increased. Some punishment of ourselves for having these feelings that we do not accept in ourselves is therefore in order.

*1.* Sometimes turning anger in on oneself results in *physical illness*. The symptoms may be relatively simple and fleeting. Many people, for example, will develop a slight headache following a conversation in which there was more anger than they expressed or perhaps even realized.

*Howard* Often more chronic problems develop, such as ulcers or high blood pressure. Indeed, although there is much additional research to be done into the relation of anger and physical illness, it seems clear that such emotional factors can have much to do with either the onset or the progress (or both) of most physical ailments.

The physical illness itself can then become a weapon for the expression of hostility, too. The wife, for example, who does not allow herself to express her anger toward her husband and children directly may *Mom* mete out considerable punishment toward them as well as herself when she has frequently recurring "sick headaches."

*2.* *Depression* is another frequent result of turning anger in on one's self. Marge, a middle-aged woman, sought professional help because much of the time she was in moods of black despair and because she seemed to have no motivation to do her work. Her thoughts were sufficiently suicidal that she asked the therapist to keep her supply of sleeping pills lest she take an overdose in the midst of an acute depression. As she talked, it rapidly became apparent that she had deep feelings of self-hatred stretching back into childhood, when her parents seemed to have had some need to

take a very pessimistic attitude toward her, her adequacy, and the possibility of her ever amounting to
anything. So sensitized had she become to this attitude
that any sign of rejection or criticism by others was
interpreted by her as total rejection and an indication
of her complete worthlessness.

It is not surprising to learn that Marge was filled
with rage about these slights, whether they were real
or fancied. But since she had also learned to despise
her anger, her rage remained almost totally unexpressed and not fully experienced, since to be aware
of it would be further confirmation to her of her worthlessness. Instead, the anger was converted into feelings of depression and helplessness. It was only as she
was gradually able to experience the long pent-up rage
and was able to express some anger directly in day-
by-day situations that her depression slowly lifted and
she became freer to devote energies to productive pur-
suits in her profession and in her personal life.

Perhaps the most subtle but most damaging price
we pay for the suppression of anger is in the gradual
*deadening of the self* that often occurs. The child
learns it is risky to express anger and even wrong and
worthy of rebuke to *feel* angry. Yet anger-producing
situations are constantly occurring. One "solution" to
this dilemma that the child faces is gradually to shut
anger out of immediate awareness. Years of practice
lead to some degree of "success" at this task.

In this process of cutting off one's awareness of a
significant part of one's self, it is almost as though we
were making a psychological command out of the biblical verse suggesting that "If thine eye offend thee,
pluck it out." As a matter of fact, this verse is probably
often quoted in ways that encourage us to keep our-

selves unaware of our feelings of anger or sexual desire.

Extreme examples of this tendency, which probably we all have to some extent, can be seen in advanced schizophrenic patients who seem unable to have any genuine emotional experience. It is true that such persons may occasionally appear to become "enraged," and they may erupt in violence. Even then, however, there appears to be a mechanical quality to the "rage." They are too emotionally deadened to connect their explosion with any deep, meaningful feeling.

Many of us who are not as seriously emotionally damaged as that might be described as having a slow fuse on our anger. All of us have probably had the experience of having an encounter with a person during which we feel vaguely uncomfortable. Later on, when the person was safely absent, we suddenly realized that we were quite angry. And *then* (safe again) we thought of all the things we would have liked to have said if we had only thought of them at the right moment.

In addition to damaging our relationship to ourselves, we also pay a price in our relationship to others when we suppress our feelings of anger, for almost invariably we find some way of taking our anger out on them.

## Indirect Expressions of Anger

The central characteristic of the various indirect expressions of anger is that they create barriers of emotional distance between ourselves and the other person. Thus they keep us from experiencing emotional intimacy. Since, as we have seen, we are very much afraid of the experience of love, it seems likely that we often use these indirect expressions of anger as a way of preserving the safety of distance. Evasion of direct expression of anger thus becomes a tool of our fear of love.

Looking at it from the other side, then, expression of anger in indirect ways becomes a means of cheating ourselves of what we most want—the experience of love.

One indirect expression of anger that we sometimes use is *apparent indifference*. Now, of course, if we are really angry, we are not at all indifferent. But that is the point! We resist letting the other person know that we care enough to let them "get under our skins." To express the anger directly would be to risk a genuine encounter. So instead we express our hostility by saying in effect, "You don't matter to me."

One man recalls that, as a child on certain occasions when he felt angry, hurt, and frustrated by some of his mother's stipulations, he would shout through tears, "I don't care! I don't care!" One can guess that those were rather unsuccessful attempts to appear indifferent!

*Grievance collecting* is another indirect expression of anger in which we store up anger for future use, particularly at times when there is danger of the intimacy we fear. So, for example, one woman often countered any expression of love from her husband with something like, "Well, you should have thought of that six years ago when you were off getting drunk in some bar when our baby was being born!" And this particular weapon in her grievance arsenal is so effective and important that she may never let herself be aware that her husband was so "shook up" by his caring for her and by the possibility of becoming a father (and experiencing love for his child) that he could not face his emotions at that moment.

Often our grievance collecting takes less dramatic, but just as effective, form. We may have an almost inexhaustible supply of minor resentments. Probably it would be hard for us to put them all into words if we tried, but they provide enough impetus to keep us almost constantly irritable or moody with the other person without bringing about the explosion that might clear away the tension between us and permit some frightening moments of closeness.

*Attitudes of superiority* provide another way of expressing anger indirectly. It is quite hostile after all to say to another person, in effect, "I am so much better than you that any opinions or feelings you may have count for nothing." And when such superiority feelings are used cleverly, such as portraying oneself as condescendingly tolerant of another, they become a powerful and cutting weapon.

Many men who feel themselves to be trained in logic and the scientific method use this distancing device with great effectiveness. Such a man will convey the feeling to his wife that there is something suspect about any emotional reaction she may have. "After all," he says, "you have to approach life rationally. You're letting your emotions influence your judgment."

And, of course, the wife may turn the tables and adapt her own superior attitude and say, "Well, I was just reading in a book the other day that it's important and right to show our emotions. So there!" (Well, of course she's right, but she's using it in a vicious way!)

Sometimes we express hostility indirectly by *misplacing our anger*. We may nag and express irritation about many little things, while avoiding the genuine anger which we are afraid to reveal. For example, a wife might "bitch" continually about her husband's sloppy appearance and mannerisms, when she is really angry about his lack of advancement in the company organization.

Sometimes we misplace our hostility to other people. Often this involves a "pecking order" in which we misplace anger from a person who is a considerable threat to us, like a spouse or a boss, and place it on someone less threatening, like our children, who in turn may pull the cat's tail or kick the dog!

We sometimes express anger indirectly by *projecting it onto another person and seeing that individual as being hostile toward us.* This process, too, serves the purpose of maintaining emotional distance, for if we can preserve the idea that another person is unfriendly and hostile there is little danger of our becoming close. In fact, the person may become increasingly unfriendly and hostile as he reacts to our reactions to his imagined hostility.

A discussion of the costs we pay in damage to ourselves and damage in our relations with others when we suppress anger cannot be concluded without a discussion of the violent explosions that sometimes occur. And the fact that such explosions do occur is often frightening to those who sense something of this potential violence within themselves. It is not unusual to feel as one man who said, "I have so much anger bottled up in me that I'm afraid if I ever let myself express it, I would kill someone."

Often this fear has little or no basis in fact. It serves as an excuse for imposing control on ourselves. We are really afraid of an open relationship in which we could express our anger freely. The fear that we will do violence is substituted to give ourselves a more plausible reason for not being genuine.

On the other hand, the fear of violence may have

some basis of truth. The fallacy of continuing a rigid control of our anger, however, is that this simply increases the inner tension and makes the possibility of violence more real. The frequently used analogy of the steam boiler under pressure is probably the most appropriate one. If hostility is permitted to build up and up and none of the pressure is allowed to escape, the possibility of an explosion increases.

The person who fears violence within himself may need to consult professional help to assess the reality of his fear and help him to find safe ways to dissipate the inner pressure. Jim was such a person. He was in construction work; and when irritating situations arose on the job he often became frightened with himself. He seethed with so much anger, particularly toward his foreman on these occasions, that he was afraid he might kill the man if he ever got carried away and began to express his feelings. The therapist he sought out helped him to talk through a lot of his feelings, including a huge backlog of anger toward his father that he had probably misplaced on the foreman. Jim also discovered that he could talk over some of his irritations with his boss and that when he did this his feeling of wanting to do violence disappeared even when he and his boss did not reach complete agreement.

# VI

# OUR FEAR OF SEX

JEANETTE IS IN HER middle thirties now. She has been married a dozen years and is just now beginning to enjoy her sexual life. As a child she was given no opportunity to understand sex is a realistic way. Her parents gave her no information. Her church was rigid and moralistic; and it taught her, or at least so it seemed to her, that all sexual feelings are wrong and dangerous and should be suppressed whenever possible. As a teen-ager she was filled with strong sexual desires that were very frightening to her. A couple of experiences of being approached by older men added to her fears.

The fact that she had feelings that made her want, in part at least, to respond to these men made the experiences doubly frightening. She condemned herself for these feelings, telling herself that she was sinful and abnormal. Early in her dating experience she met Larry, the boy she eventually married. During their courtship they had sexual intercourse on several occasions. There was little or no pleasure in it for either one. Performed under the furtive, cramped conditions of the back seat of his car, they both suffered from the fear of being caught. Both had been taught since childhood that such behavior was wrong, and that sexual activity should be reserved for marriage, so they experienced many feelings of guilt.

Larry and Jeanette married a few months after the first time they had intercourse. She says of her decision to marry, "I was sure that I didn't love Larry, and I didn't want to marry him. But I felt it was my obligation to do so. After all, I had had sex with him. So I felt that perhaps I would be a little less guilty if I went ahead and married him. And, anyway, I felt I would never be able to feel right about marrying anyone else, even if I could have found someone else who would have me after what I had done."

In the years that followed there were few satisfactions for Jeanette. The "legalizing" of their sexual life did little to improve it. Only on rare occasions did her sexual desires overpower her resistances so that she would have an orgasm, and then in spite of herself. And when that did happen she would quickly withdraw, finding even more things to "bitch" about than usual. Seldom did she feel anything other than hurt or resentment.

Nor did she find compensating feelings of closeness with others. Men, in particular, were frightening to her. Both their obvious attraction to her and her feelings of attraction to them were difficult for her to handle. Since she felt much self-hatred in many areas, she mistrusted other women too much and was too frightened of being hurt by them to establish close relationships.

It was only with professional help that she began to discover that she could enjoy her sexual life and that she cared far more for her husband than she had ever allowed herself to realize before.

If there is anything unusual in the experience of this

woman, it is probably only in the fact that she is achieving a new life in spite of her fear of sex. For, while the details vary, there are countless men and women who are frightened of sex and whose reactions keep them from having satisfactory relationships.

As has been pointed out by numerous authors, our society is almost schizophrenic in its attitudes toward sex. We do everything conceivable to encourage an emphasis on sexual thoughts and stimulation through advertising, motion pictures and television, clothing, and in countless other ways. Much of this seems particularly directed toward the teen-ager, who has also been given more freedom and mobility than any other teenager in history. Having provided this impetus toward early sexual activity, we are then judgmental and shocked when sexual intercourse and, especially, pregnancy occur outside of marriage. It is apparent that as a society we do not know our own mind. We are preoccupied with our sexual feelings and yet very frightened of them.

## From Generation to Generation

As with our other fears, the origins of our fear of sex reach back into our childhood years. As with our fear of anger, our fear of sexual feeling passes on from one generation to another as our children are infected with our lack of acceptance of this aspect of our nature.

It is likely that parents begin communicating their attitudes about the human body during the first weeks of the child's life. If the mother enjoys her relationship with the child and is free to relish the physical contact with the baby in feeding, cuddling, changing, and cleansing it, her enjoyment will be conveyed to the child. On the other hand, if her fears of handling the child make her efforts clumsy or hesitant, or if she feels disgust with breast-feeding or the child's eliminative functions, these feelings will also probably be communicated in some way.

Later, the fears are often transmitted to the child through what he must come to feel is a conspiracy of silence. Eliminative and sexual parts and functions of the bodies remain unnamed or are given childish names that will be a source of embarrassment when the child attempts to communicate with other children. Questions are frequently met with embarrassed silence, skirting of the truth, or halting, uncomfortable answers. The child is locked out of the possibility of talking about these matters with his parents in the same open way in which he can talk about his eyes, ears, and mouth and eating, seeing, and hearing. His vocabulary is stunted, and he has been taught to be afraid.

The child's discovery that his own body is delightfully sensitive, particularly in the genital areas, is also likely to arouse parents' fears and mistrust so that they react in ways that frighten the child and lead him to distrust himself and his feelings. Thus the development of furtive preoccupation with forbidden pleasures may begin.

The lack of communication that can exist between parent and child is strikingly illustrated by one woman who reported that she grew up receiving all of her information concerning sex, including menstruation, from friends.

This continued into college years, during which time—when she was nineteen—she became pregnant. She was certain that her mother would react to this news with nothing more helpful than shock, total condemnation, and religious exhortations, so she managed to conceal the pregnancy, even though she became very ill following an abortion she succeeded in obtaining.

Two years later, when she was making preparations to be married, her mother approached her suggesting that it might be about time that they have a talk about sex! The mother probably felt bewildered when the daughter replied in a voice edged with irony, "Certainly, Mother, what would you like to know?"

Many parents today who were exposed to these kinds of fearful parental reactions when they were children are anxious to make a change in healthier directions. Sometimes they demand these changes of themselves even though little or no change has been achieved as far as altering their own basic fear of sex. They are as frightened of sex, or nearly so, as their parents before them, and they are attempting to adjust to what may be a somewhat more enlightened time.

This often leads to new problems, as they attempt to appear open and unfrightened about sex. Nudity in the home sometimes provides examples of this. Parents whose own parents hid their bodies almost completely from their children rightly feel that this was a mistake that led to unsatisfied and excessive curiosity. In their attempt to be different they may force themselves to be naked in front of their children even though they are not really comfortable in this role. It seems likely that their fears will in some way be communicated to the children. In more damaging instances, where parents have unfulfilled and perhaps unrecognized sexual needs, this may involve exhibitionistic and unconsciously seductive behavior that is not conducive to healthy development of sexual feelings in the child. When we attempt to deny our fears about sex, we simply find new ways to pass them on to our children in disguised and perhaps more subtle forms.

The adolescent years are frequently very significant ones in the development of sexual attitudes. Jean, a woman who in marriage experienced considerable difficulty in being sexually free with her husband, told of being very puzzled when she entered puberty. Her father, who had been warmly affectionate to her all of her life, suddenly—or so it seemed to her—withdrew from her and seemed cold and distant. No longer did she seem welcome on his lap. No longer were there any spontaneous hugs or kisses. She remembers wondering if she had done anything wrong to account for his strange withdrawal and could think of nothing.

Although she never put it into words even to herself, it seems likely that Jean made some connection between her father's reaction and the only significant changes in herself—the change to a woman's body and a woman's awareness of sexual feelings. There must then be something wrong about the transformation and the feelings if they cost her the affection of a father who had been such an important part of her life.

It seems clear what had happened to her father. He had not suddenly lost his love for Jean. On the contrary, his deep love for her had been complicated for him by her physical and emotional development and his own reactions. It is inevitable that sexual feelings, which the father may or may not allow himself to become fully aware of, will occur in a father-daughter (or mother-son) relationship. The strong taboos that exist in society no doubt contribute to the strong fear that such feelings arouse in parents. This particular father seems to have reacted to his fear by withdrawing almost completely, being unprepared to accept and even enjoy his reactions to a maturing young lady in his home. And his withdrawal helped pass on his fear of sexual feelings to her.

It might be added that his fear of being hurt by Jean probably increased as she entered womanhood, began to date, and in general was increasingly in a position to make her own decisions. Few if any parents are not frightened by this transitional stage. And so, as he withdrew from Jean, the father may also have been, without realizing it, protecting himself from possible hurt.

The self-defeating aspect of such a reaction need hardly be pointed out, for in her bewilderment and self-doubt, caused by the father's withdrawal, the girl would be more likely to react in self-destructive ways that would deeply hurt her father.

In many ways we experience self-defeat and frustration as the result of this fear of sex that we absorb from our parents and from our culture.

## Loss of Sexual Effectiveness

Fear of sex frequently makes it difficult for a person to function freely and effectively in sexual activity. This fear is frequently, perhaps usually, associated with other fears that interfere with sexual effectiveness. For example, one man was unable to maintain an erection long enough to have intercourse. During moments of closeness and caressing with his wife, the penis would become erect. Invariably he would lose his erection just at the moment that intercourse was attempted. The fact that he could achieve an orgasm during masturbation made it clear that the problem must be emotional rather than physical.

In therapy sessions, three kinds of fears, deeply intertwined, came to light, all of which appeared to play a role in his sexual problem. For one thing he was afraid of sexual feelings, having been reared in a repressive conspiracy of silence about sex. It also became evident that he had a deep-seated fear of women. His mother, under the guise of expressing her love, had actually been very controlling in his early life. She was overprotective and discouraged any show of independence on his part. In his adult life he undoubtedly carried over from his relationship with his mother the feeling that to become intimate, emotionally or physically, with any woman opened himself up to the possibility that the woman would take over control of his life. His impotency was a way of protecting himself from that risk without having to become fully aware of his fear of women.

He was also very frightened of his anger. He was filled with a lifelong accumulation of rage toward his mother and his father, which he had been taught to suppress. This pattern carried over into his relationship with others, and particularly with his wife. His failure to satisfy his wife's sexual needs probably provided an indirect way of expressing his anger toward her. And, as always, underlying all these fears was the most basic one of all—the fear of love, with its potential risks. Inability to complete the sexual act kept him "safe" from the frightening possibility of a more complete intimacy.

As is the case with our fear of anger, our sexual fears sometimes result in a deadening of the self, in this instance to sexual feeling. The woman, for example, who has little if any pleasant sensation and for whom it is difficult or impossible to achieve an orgasm has probably without realizing it blocked out these feelings because of her fears. Sometimes the "deadness" may take the form of a generalized disinterest in sexual

OUR FEAR OF SEX 91

activity. The man or woman may be always "too busy" about something else or "too tired" or "not in the mood" when appropriate moments for sexual activity are at hand.

Sometimes, instead of a deadening of the senses, the person appears to be overly sensitive to sexual feeling. Men frequently have a problem in which they regularly have an orgasm prior to entrance of the penis into the vagina or so soon thereafter that it is a frustrating experience to both the man and woman since neither feel really satisfied.

It is interesting that, when they describe this problem, the man (or the woman) is apt to say that he "isn't able to control himself." Some men will go to great lengths to gain this control. One man told how he would recite the multiplication tables to himself during intercourse in order to minimize his sexual excitement and prolong intercourse.

Perhaps this is a good illustration of the frustration built into reliance on control as the answer to problems in human relationships. Notice the "logic" of the man in such a situation: "I will try to remove myself as completely as possible from this situation and deaden myself to all sexual feeling and thereby hope to attain the feeling of closeness I long for." Hopefully, there is a better way than that. If the man can uncover the underlying fears of sex and of intimacy that cause him to frustrate himself and his partner and can deal with them directly, he is likely to find satisfaction without numbing himself. It is often a stubborn problem, however, and may require the help of a professional therapist.

Sometimes feelings of obligation manage to disrupt sexual functioning. One young husband spoke at considerable length to his therapist about how much "work" it was to make love to his wife. It was "so much effort" to arouse his wife and carry the sexual act to completion. By some magic of mental manipulation he had managed to convince himself that sexual intercourse was a chore!

## Guilt Feelings

It is natural perhaps that fear of sex often goes hand in hand with guilt feelings about sex. Guilt is often used as a means of controlling that of which we are afraid. If, for example, a young man can convince himself that he is guilty for being aware of being sexually attracted to a young woman, he can preoccupy himself with self-punishment for his "lustful feelings" and devote his energies to suppressing them. Religion often plays a part in this, for the church has often mistakenly taught that sexual feelings are sinful instead of recognizing that this aspect, too, of man's nature has been given to him to enjoy.

If a man were free to enjoy his delightful, inner sexual sensations without feeling guilty about them, then he would be faced with the decision as to what he wished to do with them, and possibly he would be faced with the fact that he is really rather frightened by them. One of the functions already briefly mentioned, which our fear of sex serves, is that we frequently use it to avoid emotional closeness with others. It becomes a servant of our fear of love and the risks love always involves.

When we are unable to be freely aware of sexual feelings and freely accept them as a legitimate and cherished part of ourselves, we are less than genuine; and the falseness will act as a hindrance to emotional openness and intimacy.

One man tells how sexually suppressed and fright-

ened he was during World War II, when he entered
the Army right out of high school. On one of his first
passes off the base he went into a community center
for servicemen in a nearby city. Far from home, he
probably looked like the frightened kid he was. There
were few other men in the center at the time, so he
was singled out by a hostess who brought him refresh-
ments and attempted to open a friendly conversation
with him. He was so flustered by her attractiveness
and by her approach to him, and he had been so indoctrinated by his mother about the sexual dangers
lurking in army towns, that he immediately assumed
she was out to seduce him. He blurted out something,
probably cutting, and rushed out of the room embarrassed, confused, and frightened.

His fear of sex not only kept him from any physical
contact with the girl, it also prevented him from any
significant relationship with her. And at his stage of
emotional development (or lack of it) any kind of relationship would have been frightening to him.

### Sexual Fear as a Barrier to Intimacy

As relationships become more intense, fear of sex is
often utilized as a last barrier to preserve some safe
distance between two individuals.

Ron was married to Barbara when he had known
her for less than six weeks. He had been passionately
affectionate during their brief courtship, although they
did not have intercourse. As soon as the marriage
ceremony took place, Ron immediately seemed almost
completely uninterested in any physical contact, a very
frustrating and puzzling experience for his wife. On
rare occasions when intercourse took place, it happened only because she took the initiative. Even then
he was not relaxed, and he allowed himself little en-

joyment, keeping the act on an almost mechanical level. One of his emotional barriers to sexual freedom was a strong feeling of repugnance concerning the vagina, which was very distasteful for him to see or touch.

Three children and several years later, Ron entered psychotherapy, with these problems still acutely present. It soon became apparent that, in addition to his fears of sex, he was very much afraid of almost any degree of emotional intimacy with anyone. Although he had many warm and tender feelings, he would become very uncomfortable when these feelings were recognized and responded to in any open way.

His mother had been dominating and she constantly manipulated Ron in subtle ways. His father had maintained a cool distance and had sometimes used a vicious type of "practical-joke" approach in relating to his son. He would do such things as promise Ron the use of the family car on a particular day, and then arrange to have the car in the garage for servicing at that time. If Ron showed any emotion about this "trick," his father would ridicule him in front of his friends for not being able to "take it." It is not surprising that Ron had learned to maintain emotional distance as a way of minimizing hurt, particularly in relationships that mattered most to him. So in marriage it was almost inevitable that he would make use of some means of preserving distance from Barbara. His fear of sex undoubtedly provided the handiest means of accomplishing this.

Those with a Freudian point of view might well suggest, and perhaps correctly, that Ron's fear of the vagina indicates an unrecognized fear that he might lose his penis during intercourse. But whether such a theory is correct or not, it symbolically makes the same point: namely, that Ron was desperately afraid of giving himself wholeheartedly to the relationship for fear of being hurt. Perhaps his greatest fear was that of being controlled and robbed of his individuality (or manhood) by his wife, as his mother had done. This anxiety would appear to be more relevant to his immediate relationship to his wife than a fear of losing the male organ.

## Sex Without Emotion

There are also those for whom sexual activity appears to be relatively unfrightening as long as it is essentially emotionally meaningless to them.

One young woman had a number of apparently meaningless liaisons during a period of several years. In addition to whatever other motivations she may have had, she used these affairs to support a drug addiction problem. During this time she managed to keep her sexual activity a mechanical performance involving no real feeling on her part, although she was probably successful in fooling some of her lovers.

She had never had an orgasm in all of these contacts. But then she took up with another man and moved in with him. For a couple of months it was the same as with the other men she had known. But then she began to become emotionally involved, and one evening she achieved a climax during intercourse. In describing it later, she said, "I was immediately very angry and wanted to kick him out. I felt like I was losing my identity." All in all the experience of becoming involved, with its threat of caring for the person and being vulnerable to being hurt, must have been very frightening to her, for she broke off the relationship almost immediately thereafter.

The fear of sexual feelings is also sometimes used as

a way of avoiding emotional closeness in relationships other than those between men and women. One married woman with several children found it very difficult to become close friends with other women although she recognized a longing for that kind of companionship. She did not know why she kept herself aloof until in the course of counseling sessions she revealed that during college years she had had a transitory homosexual experience that had been very frightening to her and about which she felt very guilty. It became apparent that she was very much afraid that if she became close to any woman that she would again engage in homosexual activity.

In reality, the likelihood of this happening was very remote since she was thoroughly enjoying her sexual life with her husband. What does seem likely was that she was using this fear to maintain emotional distance from other women because of her fears of love and the inevitable vulnerability connected with it.

Another mother of young children was very frightened of sexual feelings. She used these fears almost continuously to maintain emotional distance from her husband, other men, and other women. One of her most troubling thoughts was an often recurring fear that she might harm her children by committing some sexual atrocity against them. Sometimes her fantasy took the form of being afraid that she would turn them over to some stranger who would attack them sexually.

The striking thing about these fears was that they did not occur when the woman was angry, displeased, or disappointed with her children. On the contrary, they invariably appeared when she felt most loving and drawn toward them. She was apparently so frightened of the surges of warmth and caring that she felt for them that she had to find some reason to pull away from them at such moments, and she convinced herself that she was motivated by some "evil impulse." Once she began to recognize that she was afraid of her love for her children, but that she did not in reality want to harm them, she felt greatly relieved. Her fantasies of attacking them began to recede and she found herself increasingly able to express her love for them in direct ways, such as playing games with them and cuddling them, which gave her and them much pleasure. She still became frightened, but now she knew why she was afraid and, without damaging her relationship to the children and without having to accuse herself of being a "monster," she could quietly withdraw for a while when the fear became too intense.

# VII

# OUR FEAR OF MANHOOD
## AND WOMANHOOD

MUCH CONFUSION EXISTS today about the roles of men and women. We tend to be uncertain about what it means to be a man or a woman, and this uncertainty adds to the fears that keep us from knowing, accepting, and affirming ourselves.

At one time in our history little confusion existed concerning these roles, for there was a rather clear social expectation. The man was expected to be the head of the home. When a final decision was to be made concerning important matters affecting the family, it was his responsibility to make that decision. If he chose to consult his wife for her opinion that was fine and gentlemanly of him, but he was not required by social custom to do so.

Now, even in those days—some might say "good old days"!—women probably were the *real* rulers in the home more often than the men would have cared to admit. But at any rate there *was* a social standard that man should have dominion over woman.

But times have changed. Our society granted women the right to vote. Increasingly it gave them additional legal rights. In times of national emergency it encouraged them to work, and they made themselves so indispensable that many of them continued to work when the emergency was over. Gradually, virtually all professions were opened up to them. Equal educational opportunities became available to them and they increasingly took advantage of them. With all these changes taking place it was inevitable that the woman's role, and man's too, within the home and in relationship to each other would change.

But in what way? As so often occurs in times of social transition, the old ways tended to be abandoned without a clear definition as to what the new would be.

As others have pointed out, certain periods of history are characterized by particular forms of neurotic behavior. A good case can be made for believing that our basic neurosis, our fear of love, has been expressed in many of our reactions to the shifting roles of men and women that occurred in the rush to fill the vacuum created by the changing times.

Although the changes unquestionably opened the door to the possibility of new and exciting opportunities for emotional closeness between men and women never widely experienced before, we have frequently avoided this "dangerous" intimacy. Some of us reacted in extreme ways against the former roles. Others avoided the hopeful possibilities with more or less desperate attempts to cling to the old ways in male-female interaction while the world moved on.

## Woman's Dilemma

When women overreact against the old system, it often means turning to a strongly competitive role in relation to men, sometimes subtly, sometimes openly, expressed. The woman often appears to make a fetish, suggesting a deep insecurity about herself, of proving to the world, and probably most of all to herself, that she is not only the equal of any man but also superior to most. She may even attempt to dominate men as men dominated women in the past. This approach to life often leads to a de-feminization, which creates a veneer of hardness that seems to defy any man to attempt genuine intimacy with the woman.

She may not shy away from *physical* closeness, for part of her "platform of equal rights" may well include a revolt against the double standard and a frenzied effort to prove that she is as sexually "free" as any male. But her fear of domination, her mistrust of herself and of her sexual partner, may make it impossible for her to allow herself to experience genuine warmth and affection for a man.

Strong reactions against feelings of dependency are often involved. All of us—men as well as women—have desires to be taken care of, protected, and sheltered by another loving person. But the woman who is afraid she may not be able to avoid domination is very threatened by such feelings. She may go to great lengths to suppress and even deny to herself these feelings of need for another.

One woman interpreted her sexual needs and desires in this light: "The key word for me," she said, "is surrender. If I let myself go and enjoy sex with my husband, it means to me that I've surrendered some of my independence to him." She went on to describe a recurrent feeling she had had of wanting to "take a knife and cut out my stomach." In fact, she went on to describe times when this struggle between her sexual desire and her wish to deny these needs had become so strong that she had clawed her stomach raw with her hands. "I just want to cut out all my feelings," she said.

## The Male's Abdication

For men, overreaction against the old ways often leads to a near abdication of any meaningful role in the home. Convinced that he dare not dominate the home, he may abandon all leadership and leave the administration of home, household finances, and the discipline, education, and open expression of love of his children to his wife as her exclusive sphere of activity. Of course other factors, such as modern industrialization and our commuting ways, which often make the man's workaday world a vastly different existence far separated from the home, both physically and psychologically, have encouraged this trend.

The result is that, in the home, where the man might hope for emotional intimacy with a wife and children, he often seems, and may even adopt the role of, an inferior, bumbling, ineffectual creature who is a nonentity at best and at worst someone who disrupts the efficient routine that his wife has in operation when he is not around. He may feel like an outsider.

While this may appear to be a caricature of American males today, there are many who fit the picture and many more who tend in that direction—men who appear to be afraid to be genuine persons in relation to their wives and children.

Furthermore, our society appears likely to proceed further in that direction since a snowballing effect can be observed. Since family life is increasingly centered around women, it appears that girls are likely to emulate their mothers. Boys, on the other hand, confronted with a dominant mother image and a largely absent and apparently weak father, are likely to be increasingly confused about their role. They are likely to identify with the dominant mother and become increasingly feminized, and yet at the same time be frightened of women, who for them seem all-powerful. As one man put it, "I've never won an argument with a woman in my life! They're so good at repartee." Another man, speaking of his wife, said, "When we fight, she has a machine gun and I have a BB gun!"

This changing role of men is likely to lead to many symptoms of emotional disturbance. The man may express his fear of women and his (perhaps largely unconscious) rage by becoming sexually impotent. He may turn toward homosexuality, as he seeks to satisfy his need for some kind of intimacy with fellow males, who pose less threat to his damaged sense of personal identity. He may make sexual conquests with women, in his workaday world, that involve little genuine intimacy. He may even adopt any one of many distancing devices, since the fear of love is magnified by his perspective of women.

The woman, of course, is in a similar bind. For as the man tends in various ways to withdraw from her, her own protective devices come into play. Without quite knowing what is going on, she feels frustrated, hurt, and abandoned. The risks of expressing love and understanding seem too great, so she goes on her way, substituting control and irritable nagging for the love she longs to give and receive, but which she fears.

## Clinging Vines and Dictators

The situation is no more encouraging when men and women attempt to cling to the old pattern of male-dominated relationships. For the woman this often means that she takes great pride in being "feminine" and, perhaps, protests too much that she enjoys being "just a housewife" who devotes her life to home and children and is dependent on her husband for economic support, direction, and decision-making.

Very often, particularly in a world where the position of women has changed, the woman has more hostility about this subordinate role than she admits, even to herself. Frequently this rage expresses itself in a "helpless" role played by the woman, which in reality gives her a powerful tool for controlling those around her.

One such woman seemed "helpless" in many ways. She was frightened of driving into the nearby metropolitan area from the suburbs in which she lived. So whenever she needed to go it was up to her husband to take her. Her housework and shopping often seemed like overwhelming tasks, so her husband had to help out. She depended heavily on him to "take over" with the children.

Then, in the throes of marital difficulties, the husband moved out. But she found to her surprise that she could function perfectly well without him. When she needed to go to the city, she drove without a qualm. She organized her housework and shopping around a job schedule and had things running more smoothly than they had ever been when her husband was around to help.

After a few weeks of separation, the husband moved back home to "give it another try." Immediately she slipped back into the "helpless" role. She suddenly was "unable" to do what she had been doing so nicely. Finally she was able to see that she had been playing this dependent role hoping thereby to hold on to her husband because she "needed" him so much and "could not get along without him," although in reality the role made her seem an incompetent nag toward whom the husband reacted with irritability and criticism.

The man who maintains a dominant role in the home and reserves important decision-making to himself may, if he is a benevolent dictator and his wife does not mind, have a relatively successful and happy relationship. Nevertheless, the role of superiority always creates some emotional distance. You cannot have it both ways, a superior-subordinate relationship and a full partnership. And probably only in the latter can the fullest intimacy be achieved.

Little needs to be said, of course, about those situations in which men attempt to maintain a dominant position in the home by physical or psychological brutality. Emotional intimacy is absent, and if the relationship continues indefinitely the woman who tolerates it must either be too weak to institute a change or have a need for punishment.

Perhaps the central characteristic of the relations that have been described is that each of them involves a denial and suppression of parts of the self. The person may have some awareness of this, or it may occur with little or no conscious thought.

## Is Half a Loaf Better Than None?

This denial of the self is a sympton of distrust and hate of one's self. The individual not only does not accept as a legitimate part of himself that which he denies and suppresses; he also assumes it will not be accepted by those whose love he most desires. Furthermore, he lacks confidence in his ability to handle the situation if he were to express all of his feelings and then encounter the hurt he fears.

Thus, although one woman may never see what she is doing clearly enough to admit it even to herself, her relationship to her husband may be summed up as follows: "Even though I long to be loved and protected, I dare not let him see that I am warm and soft and full of need for him. Even if he responded at the moment, he would see my vulnerability and weakness and would inevitably hurt me and use me more than I could bear. I would be in his power."

Or another woman's life may suggest that she is saying: "I have to tiptoe carefully through life and not let my husband see I have a mind of my own. I have good ideas about what should be done in our home and family life, but if I let him know directly about these things he'll think I'm trying to run his life. There are ways I have of getting things I want out of him, but I could never discuss them with him directly. If I didn't keep him thinking I am pretty helpless and that he's the 'he-man' around here, he'd probably leave."

And one man's life may sound something like this: "I have all kinds of feelings, but I cannot afford to let her see many of them. Sometimes I feel lonely and frightened—like I did often when I was a kid. And maybe I *would* like to put my head on her lap and cry a little and be comforted. But I wouldn't let myself do that—let her see my little-boy feelings. I would seem weak to her, and she would despise me even though she might make a show of comforting me at the time. In fact it's even hard for me to show my tenderness and love for her most of the time, for I just feel in my bones that she would get around to taking advantage of my weakness."

The tone of another man's life may be: "I'd like to be more significant to my wife and family than I am. And sometimes I feel angry both at myself and at her because I'm not. I have some pretty definite ideas, too, about how things should be run around here, but often they seem to run counter to what she wants. But I guess it makes sense to let her do things her way. If I didn't there'd probably be everlasting bickering and the marriage might not survive. I guess it's just better to get most of my satisfactions outside the home."

Involved in all of these lives is an almost paradoxical relationship between independence and dependence. None of the persons described is truly independent; that is, they lack self-acceptance and confidence in their ability to stand alone if need be. There is, therefore, a deep-rooted insecurity about relationships and a fear that they will be abandoned by those who are important to them.

Without full awareness of what is happening they dedicate their lives to the proposition that "half a loaf is better than none." In other words, they settle for a partial relationship rather than risk no relationship at all.

Since they do not feel truly independent, they cannot risk letting others see their dependency—their need for love. Or they feign a dependency that in reality is simply a new means of controlling the other person and seducing him into staying around.

What it comes to is that our fear of manhood or womanhood is, above all else, a fear of being ourselves. For society today, if we only could grasp it, has probably opened the door more widely than ever before to the possibility of creative relationships between men and women. The answer lies in the direction of the disarmingly simple but very complex matter of being our total selves in relationship with the opposite sex.

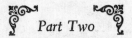

*Part Two*

# LIVING TO BE OURSELVES

## VIII

# BECOMING MEN AND WOMEN

W E HAVE SEEN THAT modern society has tended to abandon the pattern of living in which men dominated women in their various relationships. One probable reason this movement has taken place is that there has been an increasing awareness that the former way was not only unfair but also tended to deprive both men and women of the experience of emotional intimacy, one of our most basic desires and needs.

We have also seen, however, that the change has often resulted in a competitive relationship between the sexes that has been no more successful in satisfying the need for love. This is not to say, of course, that marriages based on either the dominance-submission or the competitive pattern are doomed to failure. In fact they are often very successful when judged in terms of permanence or even in terms of the relative satisfaction for the individuals involved in them, and it would not be desirable to suggest that such relationships should be terminated.

## Affirming One's Self

What is being said here is that many persons will feel that neither of these alternatives is sufficiently satisfying for them. They long for some more creative approach to man-woman relationships. For these men and women it would seem desirable to look further. The key to this search is to be found in *self-affirmation*.

When a person is able to be himself and express his feelings directly and clearly to another he has opened the door to the possibility of a creative encounter with that individual. And if that person is not too frightened by this direct approach and can respond with similar candor and self-affirmation both are likely to feel that their confrontation has been a fulfilling experience. And this feeling of fulfillment does not necessarily depend on the two people reaching an agreement. Often when different viewpoints are involved, such an encounter can take place without changing the minds of either party. And yet each person can have the satisfied feeling that he has been true to himself and that he has a deepened respect and caring for the other, who has been equally true to himself.

A certain couple, Mary and Ed, had been having difficulties in their marriage and sought the help of a marriage counselor. Conferences were set up so that each of them saw the counselor once a week without the other present. Each one had many complaints about the other. Mary's main "gripe" was that Ed always seemed half-hearted in his attitude toward her. When he wanted to have sexual intercourse, for example, Ed would approach her very tentatively as though he feared or even expected that she would reject his advances. And often Mary *did* repulse him, probably in part because his efforts did little to convince her that he really cared for her and desired her sexually.

Mary and Ed's emotional impasse had various effects on their relationship. When intercourse was agreed upon Ed could not always become sufficiently aroused to complete the act. This temporary impotency was probably related to his fear of intimacy, his doubts of

his adequacy, and to Mary's failure to respond more enthusiastically to his hesitant advances.

Mary, on the other hand, experienced times when she felt acute sexual desire and frustration that she seemed unable to communicate directly to Ed. If she had been able to communicate her desires, this might have helped him satisfy her needs. As a result of her frustration she often felt very depressed and became sarcastic and nagging toward him.

One morning when Mary came to see the counselor it was quickly apparent that she was filled with anger about life in general and toward her husband in particular and she spent most of the hour "bitching" about him. When she was not speaking of him, she talked about how depressed she was, how empty life seemed, and how she sometimes wished she could die. As she left the office, still angry, she vowed she was not going to let "that guy" near her that night. For one thing, it was a Saturday, and on Saturdays he expected intercourse to occur, and she made it quite clear that she did not appreciate such "scheduling of romance."

During Ed's appointment the next week no information was volunteered about this particular subject, so the counselor waited until Mary's appointment the following Saturday to hear the next chapter.

She reported that when she had left the office the previous week she had gone straight home, marched into the house and through it directly into the bathroom, glancing neither to the left nor the right! Ed, with that amazing sensitivity that men occasionally display, became aware somehow that all was not well! And he marched into the bathroom right behind her, slammed the door, and locked it.

With his own temper now thoroughly aroused he said something like this: "I can tell you're damned mad, and I'll be damned if I'm going to live in this house all day with you like this. We're going to stay right here until we find out what's going on!" And they did. They stayed there and "had it out" for more than an hour.

When Mary had finished telling all of this, the counselor looked at her and asked, "Well, how did you like that kind of treatment from your husband?"

At this Mary put her hand to her head in a motion of bewilderment as though she could not quite figure herself out and said, "You know, I *liked* it!"

And actually, the question had been unnecessary, for she had a bounce and a sparkle about her that morning the counselor had never seen in her before. She also reported, not so incidentally, that they had had a very satisfying sexual experience not only that night but the following night as well.

## The Hazards of Pleasing

Why did Mary respond so favorably to her husband's angry reaction? This is an important question to ask. Many might tend to say, "Well, this is domination, and a woman likes to be dominated," but this would be an inaccurate evaluation. He was not at that moment riding roughshod over his wife's feelings. Rather, he was expressing *his* feelings. He was not, right then at least, hedging about, as he so often did, in fear that he might say something displeasing to her. He was affirming himself as a valid person—a man, if you will —in the relationship. He had the "guts" to say to her in effect, "Look, you aren't treating me as a person when you get mad at me and don't tell me what it's all about, and I don't like it!"

And what is equally important to notice is that, in the act of affirming himself, he treated her as a valid person. Here was the respect she was unaccustomed to receiving from him, for he was letting her know that she mattered to him. For he was really saying to her, "I care too much about our relationship to let it rot away without fighting for it." So his angry reaction was an expression of caring.

Another question that may well be asked regarding Ed and Mary has reference to the male-female relationship. If the situation had been reversed could Mary have confronted Ed with her anger without endangering her femininity? There are certainly feminine *ways* of doing things. But there is no reason to believe that those patterns of behavior cannot include direct, open communication of feelings. And surely a woman has no less need or right to affirm herself than a man.

Self-affirmation in human relationships is much more likely to leave people feeling close to each other than the alternative of trying to guess what the other person wants and then attempting to please him. Many couples play this kind of game until it becomes a veritable "After you, my dear Alphonse!" routine.

On casual inspection it might appear very desirable in a marriage, for example, for both the man and the woman to be dedicated to pleasing the partner. It almost sounds like the Golden Rule of "doing unto others as we would have them do unto us," doesn't it?

There are two hitches. In the first place, how can we be sure what the other person really wants if he does not tell us? It is not unusual at all for couples to do something that neither of them wants to do, because they have only guessed—never really known—what the other wanted done and because each has been so "considerate" of the other person's feelings that they have not made their own wishes clearly known.

The second hitch is that if we accede to another person's wishes (or what we think they want) we are likely to have more resentment about the matter than we are fully aware of. And we are almost sure to express that resentment in some way, however subtle.

Wife Edna suggests a family picnic. "It's about the *last* thing I want to do," thinks husband Harry. But everyone else seems to be enthusiastic, so Harry says nothing about his personal feelings and goes along with the plan despite his unspoken reluctance. But the resentment is there and Harry becomes somewhat moody. He drags his feet during the preparations; and during the "happy" experience itself, he becomes irritable and snaps at the children for the kinds of little things that always happen at picnics.

Perhaps it would have been quite a different story if Harry had openly voiced his objections. Perhaps plans might have been changed or modified to overcome some of his objections. Or perhaps they would have gone ahead with the picnic with no external change. But Harry's *feelings* about it might have been quite different if he had been free to express his negative reaction and *then* decided to go. Having expressed his feelings he might well have been free to enjoy the experience.

If the Golden Rule is indeed to be applied to this situation, let it be in this way: "I am going to let those I care for know how I feel and what I desire, because this is the way I would like them to relate to me. If I do not agree with what they say, I am perfectly capable of standing up for myself. And I have sufficient confidence in them to assume that they can fight for themselves if and when it's necessary."

## Who Makes the Decisions?

Just a word may be said here about decision-making in the home, for it relates to the roles of men and women.

It appears that the most emotionally satisfying arrangement for both the man and the woman is one where there is free-floating leadership. In other words, when a decision is to be made there is no assurance in advance whose judgment will be followed. In this arrangement both the man and the woman (and the children, too, as will be suggested later) are free to express their feelings and ideas.

This makes for some lively discussions, even noisy arguments, at times! But as a matter of fact democracies are always considerably noisier than authoritarian governments (at least until the revolution comes!). And how much love and emotional closeness can be experienced between a man and a woman if a man is convinced of his superiority and a woman is afraid to open her mouth for fear of displeasing the master? Besides, is a book not more exciting and more fun if you do not know for certain in advance how it is going to end?

## Toward Independence

The creative relationship between men and women that is being suggested here calls for relatively mature and self-reliant individuals. It will be helpful, therefore, to look more closely again at the relationship between dependence and independence.

Newborn babies are nearly the ultimate in dependence. They rely on others for food, for shelter, for cleanliness, and for dryness. They are almost immobile and cannot recognize danger, much less escape from its path. They must be protected if they are to survive.

They come equipped with only the most rudimentary instinctive reactions, such as the ability to suck and an almost unlimited capacity to let people around them know in no uncertain terms that something is wrong if they are uncomfortable in any way. And, of course, much of the charm that children have is related to this natural dependency. Despite all the inconvenience involved, we adults receive much satisfaction from protecting the baby and satisfying its needs.

If the child's life progresses normally, it becomes increasingly capable of doing more and more things for itself; and therefore it becomes less and less dependent on others. Ideally this occurs not only in the child's developing ability to satisfy his physical needs, but he also becomes more and more capable of and responsible for the satisfaction of his emotional needs. Gradually he extends his relationships beyond the home as he makes emotional ties with playmates and with adults other than his parents.

During teen years this widening of horizons accelerates and parents become less and less the focal point of his relationships. Ideally, by the time he is old enough to marry, his relationship with his parents includes a sense of equality and mutual love and respect marked by a freedom on the part of both to hold their own values and views of life without needing to attempt to control those of the other.

Such a young person would be well suited to the type of male-female relationship suggested in this chapter. But unfortunately probably few of us move so directly toward independence. As we saw earlier, parents are human, too; and because of their feelings of worthlessness and their fear of closeness, they are not free to provide a completely loving, secure, and yet free home that would give the child the undergirding development of self-acceptance, which is the prerequisite of independence.

So all of us grow up with only relative ability to stand on our own feet. And if we wish to be more independent than we are, we must move in that direction with whatever help we can find. Much will be said later that may aid us in our struggle for freedom.

Our degree of independence is crucially important in our relationship with others in general and with members of the opposite sex in particular. Fence posts provide an analogy that may clarify this.

Picture first of all two fence posts that are so poorly placed in the ground and so poorly constructed that they cannot stand alone. If they are upright at all it is only because they are leaning against each other. If you took one away the other would fall down.

That is a rather accurate picture of many marriage relationships. Each of the partners was attracted to the other and they remain together because they are dependent on what the other person has to offer. Even in relationships where one of the couple seems very strong and the other very submissive, the "strong" individual is likely to be very dependent on having someone around to play the "weak" and submissive role.

Imagine, now, another fence post. This one is sturdy, strong, and firmly planted in the ground. This is the picture of a person who has learned to "stand on his own two feet." Such a person has achieved the freedom to be himself, to take responsibility for his own actions, and to meet the world creatively. The picture is still incomplete, however, for a fence post by itself is not fulfilling its function. It is complete only as it is meaningfully related to other fence posts.

This is true of people, too, if we agree that our greatest sense of fulfillment and satisfaction comes in being in meaningful relationships with other people (not necessarily in marriage) whom we love and who love us.

We never outgrow our need for love, human understanding, and communication. If we can achieve a relatively high degree of personal independence, then we will be free to satisfy these needs in mutually fulfilling relationships with others. If we have confidence in our abilities to be relatively free and able to disentangle ourselves if we feel others are attempting to manipulate and control us, it will be less frightening to us to say in the many ways that it can be said openly and clearly, "I love you, and I need and want your love."

## The Creative Individual

How can all this be summed up in relationship to manhood and womanhood? Are there any values that can be stated that will give us some direction?

It is risky to do so, because it is always dangerous to set up standards. One danger is that we will judge ourselves and others by them. They may thereby become a tool of our self-hate rather than something for our thoughtful consideration and encouragement. There may also be a risk in seeming to advocate conformity—a new kind of mold in which all must fit to be acceptable. Yet surely if we move in the direction of greater personal freedom, the freedom will express itself in the discovery of creative individuality.

So, despite these risks, some qualities of mature manhood and womanhood, as seen with our limited vision, can be summarized:

A man does not need to be a bully either physically or psychologically. He does not have to dominate those around him or have his way all the time. Those who exhibit such needs are basically insecure about their masculinity, constantly trying to convince themselves and others that they are "real men."

A man is self-affirming and independent. He can express his feelings directly and fight for himself when need be. His independence also makes it possible for him to see others' viewpoints and change his mind when it seems appropriate to do so.

A man can afford to be gentle, for his self-confidence is deeply based and not dependent on maintaining some "manly" pose. The advertising slogan "tough, but oh, so gentle" may describe him well. He is not too frightened to share his feelings of love, hurt, discouragement, and desire for love.

A woman has opinions of her own and is an individual in her own right, not a pale shadow of her husband. She can express her ideas and fight for them when need be.

A woman does not need to be a driving competitor to her husband. She does what she does because she enjoys it and finds fulfillment, not because she has to prove her worth; for she already has confidence in that.

A woman can be loving, cuddly, and soft without being a whimpering, "spineless," dependent creature who uses her "helplessness" to control people around her and get what she wants from them. Like a man, she is not too frightened to share her feelings of love, hurt, discouragement, and need for love.

Perhaps more than ever before in history our society has opened the door to the kind of relationship between men and women that is envisioned here. We have the opportunity of genuine intimacy between those who have been educationally prepared to talk the same language and share many of the same concerns. To become the kind of men and women who can achieve this is a difficult task that we will never perfectly achieve. But the adventure of moving in that direction is an exciting one!

# IX

# THE CREATIVE USE OF ANGER

WE HAVE ALREADY seen that we are frightened of the anger within us, because we have been taught to fear it and to consider its direct expression to be evil and dangerous. We have also seen that chronic suppression of anger does damage to ourselves and to our relationships with others. It is time now to look at the positive side in order to see that anger is a natural and legitimate part of our lives and that it has creative uses in our relationships with others.

Perhaps the naturalness of anger can best be observed in small children who have not yet learned to suppress their feelings. In its most pure form, anger is a reaction to frustration of desire. Thus, if a playmate grabs Johnny's valued toy and runs off with it, Johnny becomes angry and yells or attacks, or both. If an adult enters the scene at that moment, seizes the angry child and pinions his arms at his side, Johnny is then likely to become angry with the adult; for now he has not only been frustrated in his desire to play with his toy, but he has also been deprived of his freedom to do what he wishes about it, constituting further frustration.

As is the case with adults, too, children's natural

response of anger is often coupled with other emotions. If he is threatened by a bully he will feel frightened, but he is also likely to feel angry, too. If the fear is strong enough to keep him from attacking, he may feel a helpless rage. His fear tells him to run and his anger tells him to attack. Momentarily, at least, he is immobilized. Although adult situations are usually more subtle and sophisticated than this, similar feelings are common.

Hurt, too, is often accompanied by anger. If the bully attacks and bloodies the child's nose, there will be anger as well as pain. If the threat is not removed the child will also fear further hurt. Most often for the adult—and often for the child, too—the pain that is experienced will have been inflicted psychologically rather than by physical injury, but the principle is the same.

Certain automatic bodily reactions are the natural accompaniment of the emotion of anger. These probably differ very little from those that occur when we become frightened. These changes in the body serve the practical purpose of preparing the individual to meet the emergency situation at hand.

What happens to Joe Doaks when he becomes angry? If Joe's stomach is at work, that digestive process slows to a virtual halt. The blood supply in those regions and in the skin is sharply reduced and this supply rushes to the muscles and to the brain, where the body assumes it will be needed. His heart beats faster and blood pressure rises. Meanwhile, the adrenal glands have pumped adrenaline into the blood stream, which causes certain chemical changes to take place. Sugar is released into the blood stream, and more oxygen becomes available, increasing the potential output of energy. Changes also occur to provide for more rapid clotting of the blood than usual if a physical wound is suffered. In a dramatic way the body has prepared itself for action. If Joe decides to fight, his body is ready. If he decides to run away, his body is ready for that, too! And so Joe probably really *can* run faster if he is being chased across a meadow by a rampaging bull than he could if his emotions, fear in this case, were not creating changes in his body.

So it is natural that on occasion we become angry and our bodies react with natural and automatic changes. It is in relation to people we care for, however, that we often find it most difficult to accept our anger as natural and legitimate. "Granted," we say to ourselves, "that it is O.K. for me to get mad at people who mean nothing to me, but surely it's not right for me to get angry with someone I love."

But this reasoning we use on ourselves does not hold up under close examination. It persists only because we have been infected with the teaching that love and anger cannot coexist. It rests on the assumption: "If you're angry at me, you must not love me."

In reality the opposite is probably more nearly correct; "If you're *never* angry at me, you must not love me." For anger is inevitable in relationships that matter to us. If someone whom we care for is sarcastic to us, the sarcasm cuts deeper. If one we love hurts us, the pain is more acute. And if we are frustrated in our desires by a person we love, the loss is more deeply felt. The likelihood of an angry reaction is therefore increased.

Furthermore, the more emotionally intimate we are with a person the more certain it is that anger-producing situations will arise. Intimacy includes the expression of needs and desires, and these are never completely parallel for any two people. So our desires will often clash with those of a person we love, and one or both of us will be frustrated. Some anger is bound to occur as a result of the frustration.

If, as sometimes happens, a man and wife claim never to have had an argument or a fight during their marriage, they must be: (1) newly married; (2) dishonest; (3) very insensitive to their feelings; or (4) very emotionally distant from each other. In addition they have missed a lot of fun!

## Anger's Value

If a person is to be creative in his use of anger, two basic conditions need to prevail. In the first place he needs to be aware of anger and accept it as a valued part of the self. Secondly, he needs to be able to express his anger directly and responsibly. If these conditions can be met in some degree, various values can be achieved.

For one thing, this *creative use of anger will mean less punishment of ourselves*. We will not be so likely, for example, to suffer physical illness. It is unquestionably true that many instances of heart trouble, high blood pressure, and ulcers (to name the most obvious problems) are related to the suppression of anger. When a person is filled with chronic unexpressed hostility (of which he may or may not be aware), the body is overworked by being in an almost constant state of preparation for emergency in which the heart works harder, the blood pressure rises, and digestive processes slow down. Eventually the body is likely to suffer permanent physical damage under this strain. If the person is able to deal with anger as it arises and "gets it out of his system," however, the natural rhythm of the body can be maintained as the reactions caused by the anger quickly subside.

Since depression also often results from turning anger in on oneself, creative expression of anger can frequently eliminate this punishment we inflict on ourselves. Riva, a college girl, made an almost successful suicide attempt by taking a large number of sleeping pills. In the weeks that followed, with the encouragement of a therapist, she began to express some of the anger toward her parents that she had previously felt she dare not talk about. Riva's depression quickly subsided, aided in part by the fact that her parents accepted her feelings much better than she had thought they would.

The *creative expression of anger not only helps us to be less self-destructive, but it also makes for more effective relationships with others.* Many of us, because of early teaching, go through our lives assuming the opposite. If we become angry, we are likely to feel guilty because we feel we have destroyed something between ourselves and the other person. So instead of improving ourselves in the skill of expressing anger, we try to become better at controlling and suppressing it. How can "getting mad" at others improve our relationship with them?

Well, for one thing, *when we express anger, we are more emotionally honest in our relationships.* Too often we do not really know each other, even when we desire to be intimate. Our encounters with each other have a shadowy, unreal quality, because there are so many gaps in our communication. We hide many of our feelings.

Often the feeling we hide is anger. And when we do not express our anger to those who matter to us, we do both ourselves and them a disservice. Our lack of candor perpetuates the psychological distance that exists in the relationship and cheats us of satisfying experiences of intimacy.

One couple discovered after fifteen years of marriage that the wife had harbored resentment about a pet peeve for most of that time. Whenever they went out for an evening or weekend with other couples, she thought he did not pay their share of the costs. But she never expressed her anger. Finally, when it did come out in a group-therapy session, she discovered that all the time he had been contributing their share or more in a quiet, unassuming way. If she had been more emotionally honest and had been able to express her anger years earlier, this particular cloud would not have impaired their relationship.

It begins to become clear, then, that *to show anger is often an expression of love and concern,* a way of saying, "You matter to me." On a community level, for example, significant social reforms have usually occurred in situations where someone has expressed anger about existing conditions, saying in effect to some segment of society, "You're hurting yourself and all of us by what you are doing."

## Anger and Love

The creative relationship of anger and love is even more evident in our dealings with those we care for. One woman, while talking about her childhood experiences, said, "I wish my parents had gotten mad at me for some of the things I did as a kid. Then I would have known that I mattered to them."

Another woman described an incident with her husband this way: "He got awfully angry with me last night. More than he ever has before in our married life. It made me feel angry and hurt, too, and I cried a lot. But you know, I really felt warm and loving to him afterward, though I'm not quite sure why."

It is clear that anger and love are not opposites, as we often assume. Anger says you care enough to become emotionally involved. And when we suppress anger, we often give the other person the feeling that we do not really care.

*Expression of anger is also creative because it often clears the way for us to become aware of other feelings, especially hurt and love.*

There is an interesting sequence of paragraphs in the section of the New Testament that was used earlier to illustrate the anger of Jesus. The angry words go on, and on, and on: "You . . . play actors . . . you blind leaders . . . you blind fools . . . you utter frauds . . . you serpents, you viper's brood . . ." (Phillips) But when the anger is spent, the hurt and love flood into awareness. You can almost see Jesus' features soften and hear the tears in his voice as he says, "Oh, Jerusalem, Jerusalem! You murder the prophets and stone the messengers that are sent to you. How often have I longed to gather your children round me like a bird gathering her brood together under her wings . . . and you would never have it." (Phillips)

Whether or not this sequence of Jesus' words is historically accurate, it is psychologically true to life. For when we can express anger we become freer to discover our deeper feelings.

Some of the most dramatic events which occur in group therapy follow this pattern. Participants in most such groups are encouraged to be aware of their emotional reactions to each other. Often there are feelings of anger, and if this anger is expressed directly, sometimes even shouted, a sequence of feelings frequently follows. When the anger has been expressed, the person often becomes aware of feelings of hurt, which underlie most anger. Perhaps tears flow. And finally, after the anger and hurt, awareness comes that feelings of love are also present.

Thus the expression of anger often opens the door to the experience of love. This sequence of feelings provides an explanation for the not uncommon experience of couples who report that some of their most intense feelings of love and intimacy occur after their fights when they "make up."

So we see that *the creative expression of anger often leads to more satisfying love relationships*. When we conceal our anger from others and from ourselves, we limit our capacity to love, for we are denying one facet of love.

On the other hand, when we express our anger in honest directness, we are permitting ourselves to be seen as we really are at that moment. Sometimes others will not be able to respond as freely with their feelings and the experience of love will be limited as a result. But at least we will have opened a door in the wall that separates us, which will provide the opportunity for a more emotionally intimate relationship.

Here, as elsewhere, of course, we are afraid of the experience of love. To express anger, and then to be aware of our hurt and our love, increases our vulnerability. So to express anger creatively inevitably means a lowering of our defenses against being hurt. And that is frightening. So despite our hunger for the love that might well be experienced through revealing our anger, it may well be that our fear of love is the most basic reason why we shy away from expressing anger.

Perhaps it is appropriate to attempt now to give some suggestions by which we can move in the direction of more creative use of anger. But it is a risky venture. For the danger exists that we may attempt to turn them into rules and become so self-conscious and analytical that we become even less spontaneous than we now are in our encounters with others. If this happens, the value of the suggestions will be lost.

With that warning and with the additional comment that many find they can achieve some of the goals described more effectively if they consult a professional counselor, the following suggestions are made.

## Gaining Awareness

One of the first steps many of us may need to take toward the creative use of anger is *to become aware of our anger*. As has already been noted, many people develop some degree of numbness to their awareness of anger. Some progress needs to be made in reawakening this awareness before anger can be used creatively. How can this be done?

It is often helpful if we can examine the process by which we become deadened to anger. The key often lies in our relationship with our parents. One young man, Tom, had particular difficulty in being aware of and expressing anger toward women. When he examined the relationship that had existed between himself and his mother, it became apparent that she had constantly manipulated and controlled Tom's life in many ways as he was growing up. It would be natural, of course, that he would feel much frustration and anger as a result. But he remembered that, if he expressed any negative reaction or rebelled against this control in any way, she would react with such hurt and disappointment in him that he would feel very guilty. Gradually, Tom, even as a child, built a psychological defense against this intolerable situation; he no longer *felt* his anger when she manipulated him. It was only as Tom was able to remember many of these events of his "life with mother" and was able to experience and express some of the anger pent up since childhood that he became capable of realistic and open relationships with women in his adult life.

Sometimes when we allow ourselves to experience long-buried anger and resentment from our childhood, it results in strained relationships between ourselves and our parents, if they are still alive. But it does usually seem necessary and desirable to deal with these feelings directly when they boil to the surface; and if the individual can stick with it, a new relationship built on honest reactions and an awareness of our common human failings may emerge from the wreckage of the old, unsatisfying, and unrealistic relationship.

It also will often help us to awaken to our feelings of anger if we can act on and express whatever awareness of anger we do have. For example, if a person gains the courage to talk about the slight irritations that he feels, the freedom to do this gives him confidence to become aware of more intense feelings. Once the process is started, the relief is so great that anger floods into awareness with increasing ease.

Some people who are relatively dead to their anger react almost immediately to anger-producing situations with some physical symptom. Skilled therapists, for example, will often recognize a clenched fist, a tensed body, or a foot making a kicking motion, or a sudden depressed attitude as a probable sign of anger of which the person has not allowed himself to be fully aware. Sometimes we can use such symptoms to help ourselves recognize our anger.

One therapist discovered that he himself sometimes would very quickly develop a headache when talking to clients. By examining these occasions more closely he discovered that they occurred when unrecognized anger toward the client was building up. Once he had discovered this, he found that when such headaches developed he could examine his feelings and let the anger come into focus where he could deal with it directly. Once the anger was recognized and expressed, the headache would quickly disappear.

Sensitivity to our anger may also be enhanced if we examine the possibility that we may project our feelings of anger onto others. As we have already seen, all of us have some tendency to read into others the feelings that we are reluctant to recognize and accept in ourselves. Very often when we feel that someone dislikes and resents us, we will discover, if we can face it, that we resent *them*.

For example, a mother might react very firmly to a child's outburst against her request that he carry out the trash. She might feel that he carries a resentful grudge about this task, hating her for limiting his freedom to go out and play. In reality he, having had his outburst, may quickly forget the incident. If the mother were able to recognize it in herself, she might discover that *she* resents *him* for seemingly limiting her freedom and keeping her "trapped" in the home.

Jim had been in psychotherapy for several months when one day he expressed the idea that his therapist was angry at him. He was asked to play the role of the therapist and express that anger. As he "became" the therapist and talked to a pillow in another chair, which represented himself, Jim said, "I'm angry and impatient with you. I feel like giving you a good kick in the ass so you'll get to work and we can get somewhere in therapy!"

The therapist then said to him, "Now will you be

yourself and try saying the same thing to me." At first
Jim looked at the therapist in some surprise, then a
little gleam of awareness began to appear on his face.
"Yeah," he said, "maybe I am a little angry and impatient with you. You sit there and look wise and don't
seem to do a damn thing for me. I think I do feel like
giving you a kick in the ass so you'll get to work and
help me get somewhere in therapy!" After he finished,
Jim's face lighted up with a grin of pleasure and satisfaction that he had been able to be aware of and express the hitherto unrecognized anger. It was an important step forward for him, and it happened because
he was helped to experience his projection. Like many
projections, it was based on some truth, also, for the
therapist admitted to Jim that he had felt some im-
patience toward him, which he had not expressed.

It may also help us become aware of our anger if we
ask ourselves if we are feeling angry at the right people
and for the real reasons. For sometimes we mask from
others and from ourselves our real anger by feeling irritation about less threatening things. Sometimes we do
this by getting angry at people who are less threatening
to us. We may "bitch" at the wife and kids, for example, when we cannot face and deal with our anger at
the boss.

Or we may nag the wife about leaving dishes in the
sink or not keeping the house straightened rather than
recognize and deal openly with the fact that we are
angry and hurt because she does not express her love
for us as much as we would like. To recognize and
express this basic anger and hurt would be to reveal
our deep need of her and make us feel very vulnerable.
Our fear of love makes such an expression of anger
seem very risky. It is much safer to be aware only of
last night's dishes!

So when we become disproportionately angry about things that, if we are honest, must be viewed as relatively inconsequential, it may help to ask ourselves what it is we are *really* angry about.

## Expressing Anger

But when we are aware of anger, what then? It would appear that the most natural and spontaneous thing to do would be to express it. But many of us find it difficult to be spontaneous at such moments. It may be desirable for us to examine *some of the· reasons we give ourselves for not expressing anger.* Here are some of them:

"*I may say a lot of things I don't mean, and then I'll feel terrible about it afterward.*" What seems more likely is that we will say things we really *do* mean and don't accept in ourselves. If we say in anger, "I wish I had never met you," or even, "I wish you were dead," we may at that moment *really* feel that way—or at least *part* of us feels that way. It does not mean that five minutes or five hours later we may not be holding each other and intensely feeling our love for each other.

"*If I let myself get angry I might kill someone.*" Often we use this fear as an excuse because we fear the close involvement of anger. If this fear persists and the person finds he cannot loosen up and gradually express more of his anger, he should seek professional help, for suppressing anger increases, rather than decreases, the danger of violence.

"*I'm afraid I'll damage my children's lives if I get mad at them.*" When you are angry at them the only alternative to expressing it is some form of phoniness. They can be trusted to handle your genuine feelings more than you think they can.

*"I'm afraid my anger isn't justified."* Perhaps you *are* under some mistaken impression, but how are you going to find that out if you stew in silence and do not talk about your feelings?

And so we come to the knotty question, "How can we be creative in the expression of anger?" Perhaps it can be stated as a general principle that *anger is creative when a maximum of communication occurs with a minimum of destructiveness toward oneself and others.* Like most other values, this ideal is one we will never achieve completely. But the ideas that follow may help us to grow toward it.

### Dealing with Anger Immediately

Many of us have developed long fuses to our anger. We have learned to wait until later, probably when we are no longer with the person, to be aware that we are angry. But as we become more able to accept these feelings and more confident about expressing them, the fuse becomes shorter. Dealing with anger right away will save us the wear and tear of carrying it around and will give both parties a chance to react while the situation is fresh.

If married couples, for example, could follow the biblical suggestion not to let the sun set on their anger, it would be a good thing. On the other hand, it might quickly become a ritual to help them avoid intimacy if, for example, bedtime became a time to search through their experiences of the day looking for outstanding irritations. There are probably more fun ways of ending most days!

### Noncondemning Anger

It is tricky to suggest that we express anger without being condemning, for there is a subtlety here that

almost defies description. Words used do not always
seem to be a safe criteria. Some couples, for example,
can in moments of anger call each other all kinds of
names and come out of it feeling refreshed and
neither condemned nor unloved. Others can be much
more controlled in their choice of words and yet
carry the feeling that they are condemning each other
as worthless.

And all of us have probably seen unsophisticated,
but affectionate, mothers who in a moment of exasperation could give a child a swat on the rear and say,
"Get out of here, you stupid no-goodnik, and let me
get my work done," without raising any question in the
child's mind about being loved.

Sarcasm is a frequently used, indirect expression of
anger that carries the feeling of condemnation since it
implies contempt for the other person. Suppose, for
example, that wife Madge replies sarcastically when
husband Jack says to her, "I'm just so tired of the way
things are between us that I sometimes feel like pack-
ing up and moving out." Her reply is, "That's just fine.
You pack up your damn crap and get out, 'cause I just
couldn't care less!"

Madge's response would be difficult for Jack to deal
with creatively even if he did not become very upset
by the contempt in Madge's comment. For by being
sarcastic Madge has managed to protect herself by
concealing all of her feelings except the hostility. She
has not allowed him to see that it does matter very
much to her, as it undoubtedly does, whether he stays
with her or leaves.

## Undemanding Anger

Often we muddy up the swift, bright waters of anger
by inserting demands into the situation. Lacking con-

fidence in ourselves and the other person to deal creatively with feeling, we attempt to impose control on
that person. At such times we often imply something
like, "If you ever do that again, I'll punish you [by
leaving you, by not having anything to do with you,
etc.]."

Perhaps there are times when it is necessary or desirable to issue a clear ultimatum of some kind. If a
person means it and is willing to carry out the threat
and is not attempting to manipulate the other, it may
be a self-affirming expression. But ultimatums go far
beyond the simple expression of anger, and fighting
with those we care for will usually be more creative if
demands are not present.

Again it needs to be pointed out that there are
subtleties involved. There appears to be an unspoken
communication that often occurs between people that
makes words mean different things. For example, if
some women say to their husbands in anger, "Dammit,
I don't ever want you to do that again," neither they
nor their husbands will experience it as an attempt
to control. Their total relationship says otherwise,
whereas coming from some other women it might be
experienced as a threat to the man's freedom.

## Anger That Doesn't Stifle Others

It is hardly creative use of anger if a woman feels free
to blow up at her husband at any provocation and then
becomes a frightened, quaking, disaster area if he
raises his voice. Nor is the husband any more effective
who rants and rages, bullying his way through family
life, too insecure to let anyone else voice their angry
feelings.

*Anger That Frees Other Emotions*

It sometimes happens that, when an individual has been repressed for most of his life in the awareness and expression of anger, and then becomes free to have this experience, he appears to feel almost nothing except anger in his relationships with others. He seems, for the moment at least, to be cut off from other feelings that are also important, such as feelings of hurt, warmth, tenderness, and love.

What happens is that we often mask these other feelings by expressing only our anger or by seeming to be angry when that is not our basic feeling at all. When we do this it is probably because we feel less vulnerable expressing anger. Genuine anger is a way of letting another person know we are involved with him. But to let him know that he has hurt us is to go a step farther and say to him in effect, "I am not invulnerable to what you say and do. I can be reached. And you know now how to do it." And finally, to express love is to venture out even farther on the limb of vulnerability.

When we become angry with someone with whom we are closely involved, it can almost be assumed that some degree of hurt and caring is also present. If we are unaware of these feelings it is probably because of our fear of love and the vulnerability involved. Often the natural sequence of these feelings, if not inhibited, is to be first aware of the anger. When that is expressed the hurt comes into awareness. If the hurt is expressed the awareness of love often comes to the fore.

## Admitting Mistakes

It was suggested earlier that it is not usually helpful to withhold anger for fear that our anger is based on misinformation or misinterpretation. This does not mean that we should shut our eyes to our mistakes and remain blindly angry.

There will often be occasions when we will be mistakenly angry. Someone will say something, for example, that is intended innocently but which we interpret as a hostile slam against us, probably because of our own self-hatred. If we suppress our anger, we will brood about the situation and a barrier will exist between ourselves and the other person. If we express our anger, however, then the difficulty is out in the open. Then the other person has the opportunity to say, "I didn't mean it that way at all." Then, if he really convinces us, we can admit that we jumped to a conclusion and the incident can be forgotten without a breach of the relationship.

Sometimes when we feel angry we will suspect our anger is based on a misinterpretation. And yet it still bothers us. The best approach, as in other situations, is to express *all* our feelings, not just the anger. Thus we might say something like this: "I may be reading you completely wrong, but that comment you made as you were leaving this morning has really been bugging me."

To be able to recognize, and let others know that we recognize, that we are prone (like everyone else) to misunderstanding others will often open the door to more creative resolutions of anger. Very often, of course, misinterpretations have occurred on both sides and a thorough airing of feelings will lead to a new understanding and new awareness of love.

Couples will sometimes go through years of marriage preserving their misinterpretations of each other's feelings. One couple, married over ten years, sought counseling. They had not had sexual intercourse for a year and prior to that only infrequently since early in their marriage. As they talked together with the counselor, it became clear that *both* of them very much desired sex with the other and that *both* of them were convinced that the other had no desire for physical closeness. Both felt angry and frustrated and both were convinced that if they showed any warmth or made any sexual advances the other would reject them. This fear was probably well founded; for with all the unexpressed anger and frustration each of them was harboring it would be unlikely that either of them could enjoy sex without finding some reason to destroy the experience.

There was a history of misunderstandings in the early years of the marriage, of course, that they could blame their problems on, but the point is that never until the counseling experience had either of them openly expressed their anger, frustrations, desires, and fears of rejection. And that expression was a necessary prerequisite for any experience of love, since they were so full of mistaken notions about each other.

## Be Angry and . . . ?

There is something more that needs to be said about the creative use of anger. Yet it is very elusive and perhaps escapes precise definition. Why can some people fight so creatively and effectively, while for others it seems to lead only to further frustration and bitterness? Many of the factors mentioned above are probably involved, but perhaps there is something more.

Very likely it is involved with the basic themes of

this book—our fear of love and our distrust of ourselves. One man in counseling said, "When somebody
hurts you, you want to hurt them back." When he
said this, he was referring to his angry exchanges with
his wife, which usually ended with no creative resolution or awareness of their love for each other.

When we see the anger of another toward us as
primarily an attempt to hurt us rather than as an attempt to communicate feelings, and when we then
reciprocate by attempting to hurt the other rather
than primarily expressing our feelings, it seems unlikely that we can achieve any creative experience. We
are most likely to fly off onto a tangent of accusation
and probing at weak points in the other person's defenses where they can be hurt the most.

Why does this happen? It is probably because we
feel very threatened and incapable of dealing directly
with another person. Our self-hate leads us to assume
that we will be overwhelmed if we allow the other person full expression of feelings without reacting defen-
sively and hurtfully.

Often involved, too, is the assumption that expression of anger means the absence of love, which is probably an unconscious reaction to our fear of the experience of love, which the direct expression of anger can
bring.

Looking at this from the positive side, it might be
said that the quality that exists when anger is used
creatively is a persistent basic trust and good humor.
This is the kind of attitude that, if a person could put
into words, might go something like this: "Here we
are, two people who are madder than hell at each
other. And while we are both saying things, which to
the outsider might sound terribly rejecting, yet I some-

how sense that he matters a great deal to me and that I matter a great deal to him."

It is that kind of attitude that can lead to the experience one man reported when, as the anger subsided, both he and his wife broke into pleased grins. "You know," he said, "I really enjoyed that fight, even while it was going on. I felt really alive and like I was really being myself. And I enjoyed your fighting back, too."

Such an attitude involves a feeling of self-worth in which one *feels* lovable and assumes the other person cares. The feeling "He's angry with me, so he must not love me" does not enter the picture. The individual is also sufficiently unafraid of love that he can enjoy the encounter of love even in its angry form. He also does not condemn himself for being angry.

This discussion of the creative use of anger should not be closed without recognizing that there will always be situations in which we do not express all of the anger that we feel. There will be situations, perhaps at work, for example, where we will choose to suppress anger. Often the results of expressing anger would not be as bad as we assume they would be. Nonetheless it is possible to suppress anger without destroying ourselves. If it appears necessary, it is best that we do it with full awareness, knowing that we are angry, choosing to suppress it, and accepting the fact that we choose to do so. Discussing our feelings with some safe third person unconnected with the situation may help us to deal with the feelings.

But in relationships that really matter to us—where we long for the experience of love—the creative expression of anger will usually be the most satisfying and productive choice.

# X

# LOVE AND SEX

THE CONFUSION IN our language concerning love and sex betrays our mixed-up thoughts and emotions about these areas of our lives. When one housewife confides to another over morning coffee that "Bob made love to me twice last night," it will be immediately understood that sexual intercourse occurred twice. In the subsequent conversation it may become evident that these sexual acts were satisfying experiences for her in which there was an exchange of deeply felt expressions of affection. Or it may become clear that she feels badly used by a man who, she feels, "thinks only of satisfying himself."

It is interesting to speculate about why the phrase "making love" has almost come to be synonymous with intercourse. No doubt it is in part a euphemistic way of avoiding saying that which we have been taught to be afraid of and embarrassed about.

But the use of the word *love* suggests that something more than this is occurring. It is almost as if we are saying, "Since we have decided that love *should* exist whenever sexual activity occurs, let's talk as though it *does* exist." Perhaps teen-agers are more honest with themselves when they speak of "making out" (which apparently can mean anything from the mildest necking and kissing to intercourse). For there is no doubt that sexual feelings and activities are not the same thing as feelings and expressions of love. We have little or no confusion about this in regard to the sexual activities of animals, for we do not usually assume that their sexual activities imply caring between the participants. Our fears about the possibility of sexual enjoyment existing apart from love are revealed by the fact that when a human is compared to an animal as regards sexual activities and is described as "animalistic" or some such term, it is almost always done in a context of "How disgusting!" rather than "How exciting!"

In actuality love is not always associated with human sexual relationships. The anthropologist Margaret Mead describes a tribal society in New Guinea in which it would be a violation of the customs of the tribe to love one's wife. The man of the tribe chooses a wife who is his sexual partner and the bearer of his children. But this husband-wife relationship is invariably marked by strong hostility. The woman for whom the man has great affection in that society is his sister, with whom he does not have a sexual relationship.

And although we have a different set of ideals about the relationship of sex and love, the fact is, as we shall see in detail later, that affection and sexual activity do not always go together in our society.

## Love's Meaning

It may be profitable first to attempt to discover what we mean by "love." Describing love often seems like trying to capture the beauty of a rainbow in a test tube and attempting to analyze it, but perhaps something can be gained from the effort. It is probably necessary to talk of love in ideal terms, even while recognizing that no relationship will completely fulfill the definition. What would a fully loving experience be like?

It would certainly include *mutual enjoyment of each other's presence*. People who love each other find satisfaction in being with each other. Delicious feelings of warmth and aliveness flood through us when we are with someone we know loves us and whom we love. One of the factors involved in this delight in a loved one's presence is *empathy*. A process of unspoken communication seems to take place in which we sense how the other person feels and we respond with our own emotions. Empathy differs from sympathy. The sympathetic person feels the same feeling as the one with whom he sympathizes. The empathetic person picks up how the other feels but responds with his own emotional reaction.

A sympathetic person, for example, might cry with someone who has suffered grief almost as though it were he himself who were grieving. An empathetic person, on the other hand, would understand the grief and respond with love, perhaps moving toward the person, holding him, and expressing his deeply felt desire to comfort.

Genuine empathy does not include the game in which a person *expects* another person to be able to sense his needs (to be loved, to be comforted, to be taken care of, to be needed, to be encouraged, etc.) without his expressing them and then feels resentful when they are not met. The often-heard complaint "He ought to *know* how I feel without my having to say it" is often a rationalization of one who is afraid of the intimacy and vulnerability involved in expressing one's needs.

Another mark of love is that it provides a *mutual opportunity for growth as persons*. Love gives the warmth and sunshine that make possible the maximum personality development. In an ideal parent-child relationship, for example, the child basks in the parents' love and their enjoyment of him. With the confidence gained in feeling loved the child is freed to explore his world in ever-widening circles and is free to experience loving relationships with others. If his growth is inhibited by his parents' attitudes, their love, while real, is contaminated by other qualities.

A corollary mark of love is that *a lover does not give or demand exclusive tenderness*. This idea will be dealt with in detail later. Let it suffice here to say that possessiveness discourages the maximum experience of love, which is necessary for the fullest personality growth for those involved.

Another quality of love that is mentioned frequently is that *love is unconditional*. Perhaps there is no better word to describe it, but this ideal is very slippery and is frequently misunderstood. Often we translate it to mean "Unconditional love means that anything you do is O.K. with me, if I love you. Therefore if I really love you I will never become angry with you or express feelings of hurt to you about something you have done." Such a definition of unconditional love would see the lover as an impassive pillow upon which the loved one could vent his whims. This is not the picture of a very satisfying or exciting relationship for either person! Yet we often cling to this ideal of love, which is a caricature of the real thing.

Unconditional love runs much deeper. It goes more like this: "Even though I get very angry with you sometimes, even though I sometimes feel hurt, or irritated, or withdrawn, or even bored, I cannot escape the fact that I am deeply involved with you in a caring relationship. That fact of love exists, whatever is happening between us at the moment."

When two people know in their bones that they have this kind of relationship, then they are more free to fight openly, to express other emotions more openly, and to love each other more openly and freely. Unconditional love, therefore, opens the door to freer relationships, rather than to more restricted and obligatory reactions as we often assume.

It is readily apparent that these qualities of love that have been described are not limited to sexual partners or potential sexual partners. They are equally applicable to parents' feeling for their children and to friendships between persons either of the same or the opposite sex. There may be some truth in the contention of some personality theorists that love always involves some erotic—that is, sexual—feeling. But be that as it may, the matter of practical significance to us here is that love is not limited to potential mates and that the *nature* of love is no different in our various affiliations; although, as we shall see, we may well have more intense love feelings in the context of a satisfying sexual alliance.

## Unequal Love

A discussion of the nature of love cannot, perhaps, be concluded without talking about what might be called unequal love relationships. Between a parent and a small child, for example, there is a natural inequality. The parent (hopefully!) is capable of a more mature love than the child and will find satisfaction in expressing love and meeting needs of the child that arise from the natural dependency of the child. The child, on the other hand, no matter how responsive, cuddling, and loving he is, remains a child and cannot meet the same needs in the parent that a mature adult could. If the parent has been and is so lacking in other satisfying love experiences that he demands satisfactions of needs that are beyond the capabilities and maturity of the child, the adult is bound to feel frustrated; for the inequality in the relationship is the natural order of things.

When a markedly unequal relationship exists between two adults, questions arise about the nature of the feelings involved. For example, a woman may live with an alcoholic husband for many years. He may contribute little or nothing to her support; indeed she may support him. He may sometimes be physically cruel to her when he is under the influence of alcohol. An outsider looking at the relationship can see a dozen ways in which she would be better off if she locked him out of home and heart. If she is asked why she continues the relationship she may say, "Well, I feel sorry for him and just can't bring myself to divorce him. I keep hoping he will get better, but I guess I really know that is unlikely to happen. And in spite of it all, I love him. I really do!"

Is this love? Who can judge? Who can dispute the woman's word that she has a deep caring for her husband? But when the *relationship* is examined, serious questions arise. The desirable things that happen in a loving relationship are not occurring here. The mutual enjoyment that marks a relationship of love can only be said to exist, if at all, on a very minimal level. It would appear that she, by staying with him, is stifling many of her opportunities for growth.

One might be easily fooled by appearances into believing that she loves her husband unconditionally, for she makes few apparent demands upon him. But it would seem impossible that she does not have a great deal of hostility toward him, though she may not recognize it, which she does not express directly. And perhaps her undemanding stance *is* the expression of her hostility, for in so doing she encourages him to play indefinitely the role of a dependent individual who does not need to take responsibility for his own life. It might well be a more honest expression of her feelings and potentially better for both of them if she kicked him out.

What prompts her to continue the relationship? There are probably several reasons. She may be so filled with self-hate that she would not be comfortable if she were not in a marriage where she is constantly hurt. Every counselor has witnessed situations in which a relationship such as the one described has terminated for some reason and the woman has almost immediately entered into a new alliance that is equally hurtful (and predictably so), suggesting that she has a deep-seated need to be punished.

Then again she may be so insecure about herself and her worth that she feels that even so hurtful a marriage is better than none. Feeling it unlikely that anyone more satisfying would have anything to do with her, she avoids the potential loneliness and isolation she pictures herself as experiencing without her husband.

Fear of love may also be a potent factor in perpetuating the marriage. Without being aware of it, she may feel safer in an alliance where the experience of love is minimal at best. As we have already seen, a relationship in which we are free to express and receive love, free to express our anger, and free to do what we want to do is frightening. Even a hurtful association may somehow represent safety to us if it helps us to feel that we are not free to experience these freedoms.

So when we find ourselves in a relationship in which there is almost constant hurt and we are continually frustrated in our need for growth and other satisfactions, we may need to ask ourselves why we continue it. Even though we may be quite correct when we say we love the person, this is likely not the real reason we continue a course of action so damaging to us.

It will be helpful at this point to recognize again that love never exists in an unalloyed form. Each of us brings our existing self to any relationship—our fears, our past experiences of hurt, our self-hate, and our feelings that we are unlovable. All of these factors enter in to contaminate any experience of intimacy into which we may enter. So it will be always true that we are only partially able to enjoy each other's presence, be empathetic, provide maximum opportunity for each other's growth, and love each other unconditionally. But for most of us even the partial experience of love will seem worth the effort.

Having examined some of the qualities of love, it becomes apparent that a great deal of sexual activity has little, if anything, to do with the expression of affection, despite our professed ideals to the contrary.

## The Prostitution of Sex

Sometimes sex is used as a vehicle for expressing hostility. The extreme example is rape. One young man became badly frightened about himself when he found that he had almost uncontrollable urges to contact girls whom he did not know in order to lure them into situations where he could attack them sexually. In therapy he discovered that he had strong feelings of hatred toward his mother that he tended to transfer to other women. The desire to rape, which he never consummated, was therefore primarily an expression of hostility. It was certainly not an expression of love, although it probably included a longing to be close and to be loved.

One woman reported that her husband never had intercourse with her without inflicting considerable pain. She would invariably be left with numerous severe bruises on various areas of her body as he virtually beat her in an act that could scarcely be described as "making love" to her. It would be a mistake to assume that this man had no love for his wife, for he gave considerable evidence that he did. But sex appeared to be a vehicle by which he expressed hostility that he was unable to deal with in more creative ways.

This is not to say that sexual relationships should always be marked by gentleness. Sexual passion on the part of both men and women often includes a violent and abandoned aggressiveness that, while it may be very exciting, may seem almost hostile. And perhaps some hostility is often dealt with in this way without harm. But if physical or emotional damage results in which one of the two is robbed of most, if not all, of the enjoyment of the encounter, then it would be wise to explore the possibility that a reservoir of hostility exists that could be better expressed in other ways.

Sex is probably often used in our society as an attempt to reassure ourselves about our adequacy as men and women. Our feelings of self-hate and doubts about our lovableness often lead us into compulsive ways of attempting to prove through sex that we are desirable.

Compulsive sexual activity based on this motivation is likely to be self-defeating; for after a sexual partner is found, we are likely to have the feeling "He [or she] doesn't really care for *me*. I'm just somebody to have sex with." And even if genuine caring does develop, these doubts are likely to continue, since we are full of self-doubts and may continue to assume we have been successful only in seducing the other person, not in winning his love.

Handsome people, especially beautiful women, often have such a problem. They make maximum use of their physical attributes to attract the interest of others. Their beauty wins so much praise and attention from people, sometimes to the exclusion of other qualities, they then conclude they are valued for nothing else.

A deeper reason exists for our failure to gain significantly in feelings of self-worth when we compulsively seek sexual activity as a means of coping with feelings of inadequacy. Since many of us have been exposed to ideas that sex and sexual feelings are evil, we develop an ability to dissociate ourselves from our sexual capacities. When, therefore, we demonstrate sexual competence through potency and attractiveness, we are likely to say within ourselves, "It is not really me that is being loved. It is this sexual thing within myself, which is not a part of the essence of me."

Sex is sometimes used more as a way of manipulating others than as an expression of affection. In marriage it frequently appears that the person who professes to have less sexual desire (which is by no means always the wife), gives and withholds sex as a weapon by which power is achieved over the partner. Thus a woman who may in other ways feel unequal in the power struggle she senses with her husband may, as the colloquial expression has it, "pussy whip" her husband into giving her some of the tangible or intangible things she desires. Such use of sex breeds resentments and counterresentments that keep sex from providing the spontaneous enjoyment it otherwise might give. Those who need to use sex as a weapon of control probably feel inadequate to fight their battles on more open grounds. Fear of anger is often involved, and resentments are expressed in this covert way.

If one tries to sort out the various emphases and controversies that revolve about sex in our society today, one question that appears to emerge as more significant than most is: "Is it possible to thoroughly enjoy sexual relationships that are not hostile or manipulative, but which do not involve affection between the two persons?"

The popularity of *Playboy* magazine and what has been called the Playboy philosophy suggest that many would like to answer this question in the affirmative, for—on the surface at least—*Playboy* seems to espouse such relationships; although on closer inspection the attitude toward women that is expressed often seems to be marked by hostility, which relegates women to an inferior role rather than that of equal partner.

Whether or not it is desirable to engage in sexual activity solely for its own sake is a question of values, which each individual will make for himself. From a psychological point of view, however, it can be stated that few if any of us are prepared for such a role, having been so thoroughly grounded in the idea that love and sex *ought* to go together.

No doubt here as elsewhere the matter of degree enters in. There is probably no sexual relationship inside or outside of marriage in which no hostility is present and in which there is a complete absence of need to manipulate. And there is probably no sexual relationship, with the possible exception of rape, in which there is absolutely no affection present regardless of how transitory the relationship and regardless of the fact that one or both individuals may fail to recognize or admit their feelings of caring.

## Sex as Counterfeit Love

One of the most interesting but often unrecognized facets of the relationship of sex and love is that physical intimacy is often used as a way of avoiding emotional intimacy. Since we long for love but are afraid to express caring, we often use sexual relationships either as a substitute or counterfeit for the experience of love. Or we may use sex as a means of driving those away to whom we are potentially emotionally close.

Sometimes this is done by sexually aggressive talk. In one therapy group it became evident after a number of weeks that all of the women were irritated with Max, a man in the group who constantly threw out sexually oriented remarks to one after the other of the women in the group. In numerous ways he expressed sexual interest in them. When it finally became apparent that every woman was angry at him and felt alienated from him, he protested that he could not understand their feeling, because he very much desired to be close to them. Eventually, while he was talking to one of the women, Max began to shake with emotion, and said to her, "Don't shut me out!" He then burst into tears. As time went on it became evident that Max did feel affection for the women in the group and that he wanted to be emotionally close to them and was capable of it. But it also was apparent that he was very frightened of women and the potential hurt he was afraid he might experience in a genuine relationship with them. Without consciously trying to, he had developed a means whereby he could tell himself he was asking for love and affection while in fact he was constantly pushing women away with his overly aggressive sexual sallies that successfully concealed his real warmth.

In addition to other motives that may exist in those who are very sexually aggressive (such as the attempt to prove one's worth), this unrecognized need to alienate people while seeming to be open, frank, and warm is probably frequently present. If a man or a woman approaches another person with a sexual invitation on very short acquaintance and is refused, he can then say to himself something like this: "I offered her [or him] my love, and she was too square [or frightened, or old-fashioned, or proud, etc.] to accept it."

And on those occasions when such a proposition is accepted, the chances of a genuinely satisfying experience of closeness is often remote. For both persons are in a good position to have the feeling "I don't really know this person. He [she] must be interested in me only as a sexual object. Therefore, I've got to protect myself by not getting emotionally involved." In reality both may be longing for an experience of love, but the way in which the alliance began, coupled with the fear of love they both have, makes the possibility of fulfillment of their desire for love remote. At the end of the evening they are likely to exchange phone numbers, which they are likely never to use.

One problem of many engagements is that the couple mistakes physical intimacy for emotional closeness. Many couples become so enthralled with the excitement that goes along with the physical closeness that they feel they love each other. Often their feeling for each other is based on only the vaguest knowledge of one another. Sometimes one or both of them may have the feeling "If he really knew me, he wouldn't care for me." Thus the amount of self-revelation may have been consciously limited. For others the revelation of the self may be thwarted without any particular awareness of the fact that it is happening. And the handy substitute of physical intimacy may successfully conceal the fact even from the participants themselves that they are afraid of love.

It is not being suggested that physical intimacy (whether it includes intercourse or not) inevitably limits self-revelation and emotional intimacy. It need not be so at all. But when individuals are so afraid of the vulnerability of love that they are reluctant (consciously or not) to enable another to see themselves as they are, physical intimacy provides a handy way of seeming to be free and open while revealing very little of one's self.

## Sexual Ecstasy

We have attempted up to now in this discussion to cut through some of the underbrush that prevents us from clearly viewing the relationship of love and sex. We have seen that sexual activity can and often does occur where there is no deep involvement of caring. We are now ready to move on to see that sexual enjoyment reaches its highest peak when deeply experienced love exists between two individuals.

The physical delights of being touched and stroked and the relief of physical tension experienced in a sexual climax are an important part, but only a part, of a deeply satisfying sexual experience. These sensations are greatly intensified when they occur within the context of intense personal love. When intercourse is preceded by both an acute sexual desire and the wish to be close to the loved one, when it is consummated with an outburst of the expression of love along with the physical ecstasy, and when it is followed by the happy and contented feeling of being held and of holding the loved one in one's arms, then sexual pleasure approaches the ultimate.

A seeming contradiction to this concept that sexual pleasure is enhanced by love occurs in those not infrequent instances when a person is so afraid of love that he (or she) can allow himself to enjoy sex only with someone for whom he has no feelings of love. But such a person is emotionally handicapped and fails to experience sex *at its best* and would be well advised to seek professional help to overcome some of his fear of love.

Not only is it true that sexual pleasure reaches its peak in a context of love, but it is also true that love is greatly enhanced by a satisfying sexual relationship. We have already seen that the qualities of love are much the same in many human associations: parent-child; friends of same sex; friends of opposite sex. But the man-woman relationship that includes sexual satisfaction in addition to deeply felt love gives this relationship uniqueness—a uniqueness that helps give the love an intensity not usually experienced in other associations.

And although physical closeness *can* be used as a way of avoiding emotional closeness, emotional closeness cannot usually be experienced to its fullest without it. If you want to test this idea, try sitting ten or twelve feet across a room from a person you love and expressing your love from that distance. You will probably feel awkward and embarrassed. How much more natural it seems when the person is sitting next to you or is in your arms.

Sexual intercourse is the ultimate in physical closeness and provides an ideal way of expressing and experiencing love. Many couples find it difficult to deal directly and verbally with the tensions that arise in their daily contacts with each other because of their self-doubts and their doubts about each other's love. Many of these couples use a satisfying sexual relationship as a form of unspoken communication, reassuring each other of their love. The ideal, of course, would be to have both the spoken and the unspoken ways of expressing love and working through conflicting feelings.

It follows naturally from what has been said that a person's ability to experience sexual enjoyment in its fullest sense derives not only from the individual's emotional freedom to experience and express his sexuality but also from his freedom to love. Since all of us probably have some fear of love and are somewhat afraid of our sexuality it is likely that none of us reaches our complete potential enjoyment of sex. It is a matter of degree.

## Four Representative Individuals

Questions may be raised about treating our fear of sex as separate and distinct from our fear of love, since sexual fears were previously described as symptoms of our fear of love. This position is not put aside here, for fear of sex always appears to involve some degree of fear of emotional intimacy. But fear of love is expressed in many different ways and some who are quite frightened of love may be relatively free to experience their sexuality and may even, as already suggested, use it as a way of avoiding the experience of love.

In order to understand how our sexual enjoyment is affected by the interaction of our sexual fears and our fear of intimacy it will be helpful to look at four representative individuals: Lois, Anne, Peter, and Eric, who found different levels of sexual enjoyment because of their life experiences.

Lois is a married women who is relatively free to express her warmth and love for those around her. Men, women, and children enjoy being around her because she is able to let them know that she likes them. Her warmth often takes the form of a sort of motherly enfolding of people; and they generally respond, for it carries few overtones of neurotic demand.

There is no question about her love for her husband; she expresses it in many ways. But in her sexual life with him Lois is hampered by long-standing fears. She grew up in a religious family. Her parents were able to express their love in many ways but were frightened by Lois's attractiveness and warmth. They implanted many fears of sex in a misguided effort to "keep her out of trouble." As she was growing up Lois was badly frightened on two occasions when she was approached by older men, one a stranger, one a family friend.

Nothing serious happened, but in each case the girl felt guilty and frightened by the experience. She did not feel free to talk to her parents about these encounters, because she felt they would react with shock and condemnation.

Lois does not rebuff her husband sexually; but neither does she really enjoy the sexual act. She does enjoy the cuddling and expressions of affection they exchange, but she still feels stiff and unresponsive when her husband caresses her breasts or vagina. She must steel herself to caress his genitals, which she does because she knows it increases his enjoyment.

She lies relatively quiet during intercourse and tries to enjoy the warmth of his body on hers. Only a few times (while somewhat intoxicated) has she had an orgasm during intercourse. Following intercourse Lois can usually achieve a climax through manual stimulation by her husband. Often this seems more trouble than it is worth to her; and she would just as soon skip it and rest content in the knowledge that her husband has enjoyed the experience and loves her.

On several occasions during their marriage her husband has had brief affairs with other women. She senses but has never made an issue of these flings, since her marriage has seemed secure in spite of them.

Professional help for Lois might be of invaluable aid. Since her ability to experience and express love is not badly damaged, she might quickly learn to cherish and enjoy the sexual part of herself if she discussed her feelings with a skilled therapist.

Anne is a woman who is very frightened of love but who is relatively free to enter into sexual relationships. When she was a child her parents appear to have had little genuine warmth for her. When she was six an adult male relative seduced her into permitting him to copulate in her mouth. This was a frightening experience to her, although not entirely unpleasant since he continued to be gentle and warm to her, which was rare in her life. She told no one about it, and the experience was repeated on several subsequent occasions.

As she grew older Anne became a very attractive young woman. She had deep-rooted feelings of worthlessness, but she did discover that she could readily attract men with her physical beauty. No doubt she felt that was *all* they could appreciate in her, for it seemed impossible for her to form any lasting and meaningful relationships with men. An early marriage was short-lived, and none of a succession of "lovers" led to a permanent alliance. Probably without realizing it she was attracted to men who, like herself, were incapable of deeply experienced love. Perhaps there was hostility toward men (as well as herself) in her pattern of loving and leaving them.

It would be a mistake to deny that Anne enjoys her sexual experiences. She reports great sexual excitement and gratification, including repeated orgasms. Mechanically speaking, there is no good reason to doubt her reports. What does seem missing is the rich texture and three-dimensional quality that would be present if she were secure enough within herself so that she could reveal herself and experience and express her love to a man. Her fear of being hurt makes this an impossibility for her at present.

In therapy Anne would have the difficult task of becoming aware of her self-hatred and discovering that she is worthy of love from herself and others.

Peter has been badly emotionally damaged in his ability to love and his ability to experience and express his sexuality. He is a very frightened man. He is frightened of all people, particularly women; and he tends to be a loner insofar as any meaningful relationships are concerned.

He is frightened of sex and has fantasies that he will be castrated or maimed in some way if he has intercourse. On three occasions, at the urging of companions, he has attempted to have sex with prostitutes. Once he seemed impotent. The other two times he was able to have intercourse, but he reports that except for fear there was almost a complete lack of feeling on his part—even physical sensation appears to have been largely missing.

Peter will probably have a long and difficult time achieving any kind of sexual or love relationship, even with professional help, since his fears are so crippling.

Eric was fortunate to have been reared in a family where the parents, because of their own emotional maturity, were able to express their love openly and directly to their children. When they were angry it was apparent and quickly finished. Above all, a sense of mutual respect marked the family's relationships.

In this atmosphere, relatively free of fear, Eric came to accept his sexuality as a natural and worthwhile part of himself. He did not marry until he was twenty-seven. Prior to that he dated many girls and had a number of intensive relationships. He had sexual intercourse with three of them. He had cared deeply for each of these girls. He has few regrets about these alliances and is not aware of any guilt feelings about them. He is thoroughly enjoying marriage and his sexual life with his wife.

Lois, Anne, Peter, and Eric—and each one of us—have different degrees of fear of love and fear of our sexuality. Where we find ourselves at this moment with respect to each of these factors has much to do with our freedom to enjoy sex. And as we gradually become freer of these fears we will find ourselves increasingly capable of sexual enjoyment.

# XI

# SEXUAL ENJOYMENT

SEXUAL ENJOYMENT at its best comes, as we have seen, from the happy combination of the ability to feel and express love and the freedom to experience our sexuality with a minimum of fear. Both of these factors rest squarely on the foundation of the awareness and acceptance of one's self. Surprisingly, in this most intimate interrelationship of two people our relationship to our own selves remains the most crucial element.

## Enjoying Our Bodies

One reason this is true is that sexual enjoyment is based to a great extent on our freedom to enjoy our own bodies. And this freedom arises out of our ability to be aware of our sexual sensations, our acceptance of this aspect of our lives, and our ability to use our bodies in spontaneous sexual activity when we choose to do so.

Mark, a young man who grew up in a very rigid home where he learned to inhibit many feelings, entered psychotherapy in search of help for various marital and personal difficulties. After some months he discovered that, among other changes, he was feeling differently about his body. He spoke of the change in this way: "It's kind of hard to describe, but I feel more alive than I ever did in the past. My whole body feels good. I enjoy seeing myself naked in the mirror, where I used to think I looked ugly, almost repulsive. And I seem to be much more aware of every sensation. For example, if I run my hand over a surface, I find myself really feeling it and usually enjoying it. If it's a polished surface, I enjoy its smoothness. If it's soft, I enjoy the softness.

"And sexual sensations are really something! My whole body seems to come alive. I used to think I had a lot of sexual feelings before when I was so afraid of them and almost hated them. But I suppose I wasn't letting them all come through, because they've never been so intense as they are now. And I'm really enjoying them.

"Another thing that's happened is that I don't very often have the problem of a quick climax in sex I used to have. I can't explain why it is, because I seem much more excited. But without trying to hold myself back like I used to, I seem to last a lot longer."

Another reason our own selves are so important in sexual enjoyment lies in the fact that every bit of our awareness of the other person and that person's body has to come to us through our senses. The freedom to thoroughly relish and enjoy the body and sexual actions of one's partner arises primarily out of one's own attitudes. Just as "beauty is in the eyes of the beholder," our sexual enjoyment is determined by the way we receive the sexual sensations that come our way. One woman, for example, may feel as though she is in "ecstatic orbit" through the onrush of the visual sensations, the sounds, the touches, the tastes, and the fragrances of sexual play and intercourse. Another, confronted with the same potential input, may keep her eyes and mouth clamped shut and cringe from the touch and the smells, barely able to keep her disgust manageable enough to complete the act. Her fear and her lack of acceptance of her potential sexual feelings cause her to block off awareness wherever possible and cheat herself of enjoyment of those sensations that still manage to slip through her defenses.

## Sensuality

The ability to be thoroughly sensual in enjoying sexual sensations appears to be a relatively rare quality in our culture despite our great attention to sexual stimulation. In view of the Christian church's tendency to be frightened of the sensual, one might not expect to go to the Bible for examples of sensual appreciation, but The Song of Solomon is full of it. Some of the comparisons may seem quaint, but nevertheless the sensuality comes through the ancient words.

> "How graceful are your feet in sandals,
>   O queenly maiden!
> Your rounded thighs are like jewels,
>   the work of a master hand.
> Your navel is a rounded bowl
>   that never lacks mixed wine.
> Your belly is a heap of wheat,
>   encircled with lilies.
> Your breasts are like two fawns,
>   twins of a gazelle.
> Your neck is like an ivory tower.
> Your eyes are pools in Heshbon,
>   by the gate of Bath-rab'bim . . .
> Your head crowns you like Carmel,
>   and your flowing locks are like purple;
>   a king is held captive in the tresses.

How fair and pleasant you are,
    O loved one, delectable maiden!
You are stately as a palm tree,
    and your breasts are like its clusters.
I say I will climb the palm tree
    and lay hold of its branches.
Oh, may your breasts be like clusters of the vine,
    and the scent of your breath like apples,
And your kisses' like the best wine
    that goes down smoothly,
    gliding over lips and teeth."

## Learning to Please Ourselves

This matter of the importance of the self in sex cannot be stressed too much. Contrary to most teaching
on the subject, sexual enjoyment will be most available
when we are focused on *our* enjoyment, not on the enjoyment of our partner.

Every counselor of married couples has heard many
women (and men, too) make complaints something
like this: "My husband thinks only of himself and his
own enjoyment in sex. He never tries to please and
satisfy me, so I get little or nothing out of it."

This is rubbish! To the extent that the husband
may indeed have a problem, the difficulty lies in that
he has never really learned to please *himself!* If he
brushes aside preliminary caressing and hurries the
sexual act he has cheated *himself* of enjoyment, probably because he is frightened of intimacy. The fact
that his wife has thereby had less opportunity to enjoy
herself is an unfortunate by-product of his failure to
fully enjoy himself, for to focus primarily on pleasing
the other person in sexual activity is, as it is in other
aspects of our relationships with others, the quickest

way to a stilted, mechanical performance that loses the spice and enjoyment that spontaneity brings.

There are, of course, instances in which men and women have pretended and perhaps have managed to make their partners believe that they were enjoying sex when they were not. The husband of such a woman, for example, might be convinced that his wife was enjoying intercourse and having orgasms regularly. If asked, he might describe their sex life as more than satisfactory. But the situation is certainly not ideal, even for the husband. And if the wife could admit her inability to enjoy sex, she might learn to enjoy it. The ultimate result might be far more feeling of enjoyment for the husband as well as for herself than either of them could have guessed possible.

In other words, sexual intercourse reaches the peak of satisfaction and enjoyment for a couple when each person is free to be spontaneous. The man feels, says, and does what is most enjoyable to him. The woman feels, says, and does what is most enjoyable to her. In effect each person is saying to the other, "I am caressing you and speaking my feelings of love to you because it 'pleasures me' to do so, not because I am trying to please you or elicit some particular response from you." In such a satisfying sexual relationship the fact that each person's excitement and enjoyment is multiplied by the enjoyment of the partner is a happy by-product of the natural course of events rather than a contrived occurrence.

This is illustrated by responses to a questionnaire in which this question was asked of both men and women: "What specific activities and attitudes of your sexual partner give you the most enjoyment?" Here are some of the replies:

"Once aroused she undulates her body back and forth and throws her arms around me, laughs and cries. She closes the muscles of her vagina around my penis."

"When she is not hurried, she takes time to enjoy the petting and sex play."

"An eager attitude of abandonment, loss of inhibitions. She wants to be satisfied and shows it by expression and desire."

"Her attitude that sex is fun."

"He lets me know in many ways that he enjoys my body. He caresses my breasts, vagina, skin."

"His attitude that whatever I feel like doing will be acceptable to him. I don't have to tone down my desire or excitement, because he will find them exciting."

In each of these statements it appears evident that the person most enjoys the spontaneous, abandoned enjoyment of the partner.

A good springboard for a discussion of this point is provided by the observation often made in books of sexual information that women are often, though by no means always, slower than men to become fully sexually aroused. Such writing also often contains the advice that the man ought to be certain to spend plenty of time in petting and sexual play prior to intercourse to ensure that the woman will be aroused.

Perhaps this is necessary and desirable advice for many men who are afraid of intimacy and not emotionally free to fully enjoy themselves. But it does place the emphasis on pleasing the woman, and sexual play may well become what seems like a tiresome but necessary duty if approached with this attitude. It is much more ideal when the man finds that cuddling and caressing are so enjoyable and so satisfyingly prolong his own pleasure and excitement that he takes his time because that is the way *he* likes it.

Sexual enjoyment will be much more available to a couple if they recognize that it is a value in itself regardless of what it means to them as an expression of their love for each other. If a couple is free to feel this way, their sexual life will probably provide a constantly changing, kaleidoscopic variety of pleasures that will serve to keep them vitally interested in each new sexual encounter.

Sometimes sheer animal pleasure predominates as they thrust out toward each other with an all-consuming physical hunger that makes for an almost violent coming together. At other times there may be a glowing feeling, tenderness, and intimacy as they take the greatest delight in every slightest touch of each other's bodies and linger in the pleasure of their closeness.

### Putting Conditions on Sex

Some individuals cheat themselves out of sexual enjoyment by making sexual intercourse conditional upon constant reassurances or "proof" of love. Ellen, a middle-aged wife, used this approach constantly. At all times she carried a mental list of grievances against her husband to prove to herself that her husband did not love her. Whenever the subject of sexual intercourse came up, she recited her list, saying, "If you really loved me, you would have done all these things. You didn't, therefore you don't love me, and I'm not going to bed with you." In the eight or nine years after she really got rolling on this course of action they may have had intercourse on the average of once every six months, certainly no more!

Ellen, like many who play similar games, had a marvelous kind of logic. When her husband did (by some miracle under these circumstances!) feel warm toward her and did something spontaneous and loving for her, she had the attitude, "Oh, *this* doesn't prove you care for me, you just want to get me into bed!" Yet, according to her own admission, Ellen enjoyed intercourse when it occurred. Intimacy must have been very frightening to her, for her to avoid it so diligently.

Most of us who play this game of demanding prerequisites to intercourse do it less "skillfully" and less intensely than Ellen. But in one way or another we often tend to limit the spontaneity of our sexual fun. Perhaps, for example, we develop some kind of courting ritual to which we feel we must adhere as a preliminary to intercourse. No wonder we become bored with sex if we go about it in an unvarying manner and give no vent to our potentially wide-ranging moods and feelings.

As we have previously seen, a sexual relationship is much more deeply satisfying when love is present, but even with a couple who love each other, awareness of love will not always be at the forefront of consciousness during sexual activity. To demand of ourselves or our partner that we act that way when at a given moment we may only feel "sexy as hell" is to place an unnecessary burden on the relationship, which will ultimately curb our enthusiasm and our enjoyment.

In this, as in other instances, where we make love an obligation and a task to perform, we are probably—without realizing it—using this means of backing off from the razor's edge of an intimacy that is frightening to us.

*Spontaneity in Sex*

It is not our purpose here to discuss the techniques of sexual play and sexual intercourse, although writing on this subject is probably helpful when it is used as a stimulus to our own spontaneity. It needs to be said much more clearly than is often the case, however, that sexual enjoyment comes primarily from our inner attitudes and our freedom to be spontaneous rather than from skills in the mechanics of sex. Without these attitudes our sexual activities, however skilled they may be, will likely be little more than performances, and mechanical ones at that.

Although we are not discussing the specific details of sexual activity here, several subjects concerning sex are of particular relevance to the central themes we are discussing. For one thing, it would be helpful if we could be less concerned about the ideas commonly held in our society about what a happy sexual life ought to be like. No two couples are alike. Each man and woman will have an individual (a somewhat unique) style of sexual activity. When two people become preoccupied with meeting certain standards, which they have taken over from society or some portion of it, their spontaneity is dampened.

For example, one couple may not be comfortable with the fact that they want and enjoy intercourse once or more a day. Their enjoyment may be dimmed by vague feelings that they must be "oversexed" or "animalistic." Another couple may be feeling that they "must not love each other enough" or that they are "sexually inadequate" because they seem to desire intercourse only once a week or less frequently. Yet they thoroughly enjoy sex when they are not too preoccupied with the fact that they are not "meeting the average" they have read about in the report of some sexual survey.

## Those Self-defeating "Standards of Excellence"

Many of our "standards of excellence" in sexual activity revolve around the woman's sexual orgasm. We tend to demand of ourselves that she achieve an orgasm during intercourse and on every occasion of intercourse. We are likely further to insist that the man and the woman reach a climax simultaneously—every time! These are "standards" that no couple can achieve, so every person who chooses to has the privilege of feeling inadequate or angry at each other or both. When, for example, a woman does not achieve an orgasm during intercourse she is likely to feel guilty and think that "There must be something wrong with me." She is also likely to blame her husband and feel hostile because "He didn't think enough of my needs to get me fully aroused before intercourse," and (another standard) because he reached a climax too quickly after entering the vagina. At the same time the man is likely to be accusing himself of "not being much of a man" because he has "failed to satisfy her." He is also likely to accuse her of being cold and unresponsive.

It is not surprising under such circumstances that intercourse becomes an ordeal and a focal point of bitterness and hostility and one or both persons increasingly find reasons for avoiding it. Sexual enjoyment becomes no more than a yearned-for fantasy. Yet, when couples are not preoccupied with such standards, many women have discovered that they thoroughly enjoy orgasms achieved through caresses by their lover's hand or mouth before or after intercourse. Other women have discovered that they find much pleasure in sexual play and intercourse even when they do not reach a climax, even as many men find that they do not always have to have an orgasm to enjoy intercourse unless they demand it of themselves.

It has also been the experience of many couples that when they relax and enjoy their sexual life with each other, whatever it is like, they find themselves opening up to more and more enjoyment in sexual pleasures that they were never able to achieve when they were "working so damned hard at it."

It is true, of course, that psychological or, more rarely, physical problems are frequently associated with a woman's difficulty in achieving an orgasm or a man's tendency to have a very quick orgasm or none at all. If such a situation exists and there is a desire to do something, it makes sense to seek professional help. It is not creative to do nothing except waste our energies in self-recriminations or in blaming each other.

It will also be helpful in our search for sexual enjoyment if we can be less concerned about the stereotyped roles society tends to assign to men and women in sex. For example, we tend to expect men to desire sexual activity much more avidly and far more frequently than women. To the extent that there is some truth in this expectation, there may be some physiological basis for it or it may be solely the product of our education and conditioning. But in any case the fact is that many women appear to have stronger sexual desires and want intercourse more frequently than many men do. Sometimes such women are so imbued with the stereotype that they cannot allow themselves to fully enjoy and express their sexual aliveness, feeling there must be something "wrong" or "unladylike" about such passionate desires.

Often we also have similar and related feelings about sexual aggressiveness in women. Some men feel their masculinity being threatened and some women feel vaguely unfeminine when the woman's strong desires lead her into passionately aggressive sexual behavior. Yet they miss much exciting fun if they let these feelings interfere! The man who is relatively confident in himself can afford to let his partner be on top part of the time—or most of the time if they prefer that position!

Our sexual enjoyment can also be increased if we can uncover the roots of our fears of sex and the feelings of disgust we experience. One of our most common fears appears to be that we will lose all control of ourselves if we allow ourselves to be completely feeling persons in our sexuality. One woman, while her husband had been away at war, became sexually involved briefly with another man. When her husband returned the marriage continued without his knowledge of what had happened. But she was so shaken by the strength of her sexual drives and by what she had done that it was difficult for her to allow herself to fully experience her sexuality even with her husband. It was only through recognition of these fears and the discovery that she did not need to be so distrustful of her strong sexual drives that she was able to experience sexual enjoyment beyond anything she had known before.

## Resolving Feelings of Disgust

Our sexual disgusts are often potential doorways to greater enjoyment because they often mask appetites that are unacceptable to us because of fears and inhibitions we have learned sometime during our lives. Oral contact with the genitals is a disgusting idea to many people in our society. Yet many men and women have found that, when they have allowed themselves to experience the disgust, the desire has emerged out of the no-longer avoided feelings. Often they have found that the mouth is a pleasing and exciting instrument for expressing and receiving affection.

Frequently an individual will engage in sexual activities that are exciting and essentially enjoyable and yet not be free to enjoy them fully because of unresolved feelings of disgust. Such seems to have been the situation with one woman, who responded to the question "What specific activities do you do in sex that detract from your enjoyment?" She wrote, "Sometimes we both do things I feel are perverted and immoral. After these times I am disgusted with him and especially with myself! I swear to myself I'll never do them again. Then a couple of months later we do the same things again." It is unfortunate that this woman feels a need to continue feeling that something is "perverted and immoral" that both she and her husband appear to enjoy in spite of her disgust.

But perhaps our fear of love is our most basic block to sexual enjoyment. When two people thoroughly enjoy a sexual relationship and delight in each other's caresses it is unlikely that they will not feel very exposed and vulnerable by the intimacy they have experienced. As one woman said, "After we've had satisfying sex, it really gets to me. I feel almost angry and like I would welcome an excuse to get mad and bite and scratch him. It's just too much!"

But as we gradually learn that it is worth the risk to open up to the experience of love, and as we gain confidence in our ability to handle whatever hurts may occur, our growing freedom to love will also probably be expressed in a growing freedom to enjoy sex.

# XII

# CAN LOVE BE EXCLUSIVE?

WE HAVE ALREADY seen that, although the intensity of love feelings may vary, the nature of love is essentially the same in all caring relationships. In other words, the experience of love is not limited to those who are sexual partners or potential sexual partners. And as we shall see in greater detail in the discussion of healthy families, our ability to love grows out of the context of experiencing love and acceptance in the family or in other relationships. When we have this understanding of love it becomes a contradiction in terms to imagine that we could love one individual to the exclusion of all others.

Love is not an isolated phenomenon. We learn to love because we have been loved and in the warmth of the experience of love we have been gradually freed to feel love and to express it. In other words, in order to love, we must become loving persons. And when a person has developed the capacity for emotional intimacy and knows the enjoyment and satisfaction of the experience of love, it is natural for that person to seek and find that experience with many different people with whom he comes in contact.

When these qualities of the loving person are seen,

it becomes evident that possessiveness in relationships is not a mark of love. It is a mark of insecurity and fear. It is also a destroyer of the experience of love, for when we demand love we cannot experience what we then receive as freely given. If a husband, for example, resents other relationships that his wife may tend to develop and if he demands that she severely limit her scope of activities and "devote herself" completely to the home and to him, he is almost certain to encounter resentment on her part. But even if he does not, how can he trust the "love" that she shows toward him even if it *is* genuine? He must always be haunted with the nagging feeling that she would find others more interesting and stimulating to be with if he did not use coercion and threats to keep her "close" to him.

## Our Disappearing Family Clans

The nature of our society today probably makes it more important than ever before that the nonexclusiveness of love be recognized and incorporated into our lives. For we live in a time when we are likely to feel lonely and isolated. For many Americans the idea of a family, in the tribal sense, no longer exists. Our mobility as a people tends to scatter us across the country and across the world, and blood ties often tend to be of little significance as far as satisfying needs for relationship is concerned. These circumstances unquestionably leave a void in many people's lives despite the likelihood that the experience of love in family tribes may have been a mixed blessing. The values of these disappearing family experiences are illustrated by the account of a man now in his forties who describes this aspect of his childhood in the following way.

"My mother was one of ten children, all of whom

grew to adulthood and raised families within a radius of seventy-five miles of their birthplace. Family reunions would occur at least once or twice a year, sometimes more frequently. If I pause and remember hard enough, I can still 'smell' the coffee and other delicious odors that accompanied the eating portion of these festivities and I can 'taste' the melon and corn that my uncle produced on his farm. And though I certainly didn't think of it in those terms then, in retrospect I think of the equally delicious sense of belonging to a large group of people who exuded a great deal of warmth toward me.

"I was a town boy, but the family relationship provided the opportunity to spend several summers 'earning' my board and room on the farms of one or the other of my uncles. It meant a broader experience with people and things. It meant proud rides into town with my uncle for supplies in a car that had to be cranked to get it started. Above all, it meant the experience of warmth and love, most frequently expressed in teasing by uncles, aunts, and cousins.

"Since I have been an adult I have learned that the life of the family was not as idyllic as I experienced it. There were jealousies engendered by unequal inheritances. There were the usual petty feelings people who love each other so often find to squabble about. But by and large I was blissfully ignorant of these matters and knowing now that they existed does not dim my remembered pleasures or cause me to discount their reality.

"Those were good years for me. I wish my children could have the same experiences, but we live hundreds of miles from my brother and sister and from any of my wife's relatives. And I think that the same kinds of things wouldn't happen if we were geographically close. The kind of feelings that existed between relatives and brought them together when I was a child don't seem to exist much any more."

The widespread loss of this kind of family experience has indeed created a void that makes the need for other experiences of intimacy a crucial one. Some have tried to meet this crisis by making the immediate family virtually a closed corporation as far as significant relationships are concerned. Although it is not put into words, a virtual bargain is made in which a couple tacitly agree that no one outside the family will be permitted to become of emotional significance. Such sealing off of the family through avoiding significant contact with others is a frightened response to a frightening world. We probably enter into such unspoken agreements because we feel "in our bones" that to allow ourselves to care for others would increase our vulnerability to the possibility of being hurt. It is probably also a response to our fears about ourselves. We are so doubtful about our lovability and so fearful that our loved one, if free to establish other relationships, might learn to care for someone more than ourselves and abandon us that we say in effect, "I will love you and commit my whole life to you if you will do the same for me."

Such a narrow experience of love based on such deep feelings of insecurity can hardly be described as a deeply satisfying or freeing experience. The loneliness and isolation are only mitigated in a minor way. And, of course, the participants, having no other intimate relationships, have no protection against the catastrophic hurt and loss that would occur with death or other separation from the one-and-only loved one.

## Our Hunger for Intimacy

It seems an inescapable conclusion that if we are to have a satisfying and fulfilling sense of completion in our lives insofar as meaningful relationships are concerned that we need to experience emotional intimacy beyond our immediate families. And not to have these wider experiences both raises questions about the nature of our family relationships and threatens them. For to expect that all of one's needs for emotional intimacy with adults can be satisfied by one person is to put an almost unbearable burden on any association. And to attempt to do so suggests an immaturity and overdependency that is detrimental to the experience and expression of love.

Even in marriage we are most happy and fulfilled if we are two independent individuals who recognize that we are essentially alone and do not fool ourselves into believing that we do not in the last analysis live essentially separate lives. To attempt to avoid our essential loneliness and isolation through neurotic dependence on each other is a pseudo escape from an important reality. As Gibran puts it in *The Prophet*, "Let there be spaces in your togetherness . . . for the pillars of the temple stand apart, and the oak and the cypress grow not in each other's shadow."

Although our increased mobility and decreased clan experiences have tended to bring us face to face with our loneliness and isolation, the net results may not be negative. If we can develop close ties with others in spite of the fears of love that deter us, we may discover there are better reasons for intimacy than those created by the happenstance of being related by common ancestry.

Three married couples formed a very close and loving relationship that has existed over a period of seven or eight years. They have probably been together on an average of two times a month during that time. Since some members of the group had a professional interest in psychotherapy, it was not unnatural that the group frequently explored their feelings about each other and other relationships in their lives, often talking long into the night. Sometimes violent feelings came to the surface and anger seemed likely to split the group apart. Each time they emerged from these experiences with deeper feelings of love for each other. Often the group's times together were spent in simply enjoying being with each other. If asked, each member of this group would say that he had experienced and expressed more love toward others in the group than he had toward any other persons outside his immediate family. And in times of crisis each probably felt as much or more emotional support and love from the group than would have been felt in past times from a family clan.

It is interesting that one of the most emphatic themes of the New Testament is the importance attached to the experience of love among the early Christians as expressed in such phrases as, "Beloved, let us love one another; for love is of God. . . ." One reason for this emphasis, in addition to the teachings of Jesus, may have been the fact that in some instances conversion to Christianity meant complete splitting up of families who were hostile to the new sect and its members. With such isolation and loneliness thrust upon them, the new converts would naturally seek to satisfy their need for intimacy with each other. They did, no doubt, have the same fear of love that hinders us, for the record shows they bickered among themselves and found many ways to deprive themselves of experiencing and expressing the love they longed for.

In a discussion of the exclusiveness of love it is inevitable that the question of sexuality arise. Perhaps the key question here is "Can the sexual expression of love be exclusive?" And the answer, of course, is, "Certainly we can limit the sexual expression of our love to one person if we choose to." There are many ways of expressing love to others in addition to expressing it through sexual intercourse. We are free to choose whatever way or ways we wish.

From a mental health standpoint it is important to make this choice a conscious decision. A great many men and women expend a great deal of emotional energy attempting to avoid awareness of sexual desire for anyone other than a spouse. When awareness of desire does creep in, they feel guilty and frightened because they do not trust themselves with the power of a conscious choice.

## Our Nonexclusive Desires

We have already examined the damage to emotional and physical health that such dulling of awareness can bring about. It will be much more healthy if we can recognize and accept within ourselves that we do—in common with the rest of humanity—have such sexual desires. Then we can enjoy the delicious feelings and decide on a conscious level what, if anything, we want to do about them.

It is surprising how many people imagine they are somewhat unusual in having strong sexual desires for more than one person. This is probably particularly true with women, for whom it is not culturally acceptable to have such feelings. But women who are alive to their feelings do have these desires, and it is often a great relief to a woman to find she is not unique in this respect.

As a culture we are quite reluctant to openly examine the fact that large numbers of married persons do not choose to be exclusive in their sexual relations. We are probably particularly afraid to recognize that any possible good could result from extramarital affairs. To do so might seem to condone or even to encourage such behavior and perhaps lead to the collapse of our monogamous system, at least as we now know it. But if that system is of value and if it is not already a fiction, then the open examination of all relevant questions certainly should not destroy it.

On the one hand it is undoubtedly true that many extramarital sexual relationships are destructive events in which the individual is using sexual conquest (or capitulation) as another way of avoiding intimacy, while on the other hand there are other instances where individuals appear to open up to the experience and expression of love in an affair in a way in which they have not been able to do with a spouse.

One of the aspects of marriage that we do not like to admit is the fact that it may not be most conducive to the experience of love. There are many reasons a married person can find for not feeling close to a spouse. There may be unspoken resentments about any number of things that have been built up over a period of time. The relationship may be experienced primarily in terms of obligation and duty so that the experience of freedom so conducive to love has evaporated in "that trapped feeling." It is probably true that these are ways in which we avoid experiencing the love that is there because of our fear of love. But be that as it may, it is not surprising that some people find they experience love more freely outside of marriage.

*Affairs Not Always Tragic*

If the basic relationship with the spouse is not too hopelessly unsatisfying and if the principals do not react precipitously, a marriage often survives extramarital affairs. In fact, it may be strengthened as the result of a new-found ability to be open to the experience and expression of love. But society's attitude about extramarital affairs often operates against the survival of a marriage. The experience of Alice, a young wife, is probably not too exceptional. Her husband, Al, an attorney, became involved with another woman—a divorcee—within their social group. Al was sufficiently indiscreet about his affair that a good many members of the community, including relatives, became aware of the situation.

Alice sought the help of a psychotherapist, who Al also saw on a sporadic basis. As soon as others became aware that an affair was taking place, Alice was besieged with pressure to seek a divorce. Both his parents and her parents urged it. Other friends and relatives said or implied that she was a fool if she did not see a lawyer and force him to move out. Her physician gave her similar advice. The force and the vehemence with which many of these people spoke seemed to indicate that they themselves felt threatened by the situation. It was almost as if they were saying to Alice, "What's going to happen to society if you let him get away with this without being punished for it. We can't afford to tolerate this kind of behavior."

Fortunately, Alice had a mind of her own, although the constant pressure caused her many bad moments in which she asked herself if she were "some kind of a nut" for not seeking a divorce. But when she did not immediately seek a divorce, things began to happen that made her happy she had not yielded to pressure. For one thing, she began to discover, through therapy, that she was very frightened of love and had never been free to express the love and affection of which she was capable. In fact, as she looked at herself more closely, Alice realized she had been difficult to live with throughout her marriage. She had been overly sensitive, constantly feeling hurt about something Al had said or done. Then in retaliation she would either withdraw from him behind a wall of hurt silence or "bitch" at him about little things that had no connection with her deeper feelings. As she became aware that she acted this way because of her fear of love, she began to become much more capable of experiencing intimacy, including the expression of love to Al.

She also discovered that he, too, was changing. Having known the love of the "other woman" seemed to affect Al's view of himself. He felt more lovable and developed more confidence in his ability to express love. And even while he continued to see his lover, he became more able to express love openly to Alice than he had ever been before. And she, through her new self-discovery—which might never have happened if Al had not had an affair—was much more able to respond with deep-felt love and was able to enjoy the sexual relationship as never before.

So eventually, while Al was still having his affair, she could send her advice-giving friends away muttering and shaking their heads, by saying in all honesty, "I don't want a divorce! I feel more love for my husband than I was ever able to feel in the past, and we both find much more satisfaction in our relationship than we ever did before! Why would I want to get a divorce now?"

Since Al now found many satisfactions in his marriage that neither he nor Alice had been capable of experiencing with each other before, and since he deeply valued his home and desired to be with his children, he, too, had every reason to continue the marriage rather than to seek a permanent alliance with another woman.

This is not to say that life for the couple was tranquil during these times. Not at all. Both of them, and perhaps particularly Alice, went through great upheavals of feelings. There were moments of torrid anger and times of anguished hurt. Most of all, there were times of fear. Alice would become terrified *after* expressing her love in sexual openness. It was apparent that the fear that he would abandon her was most acute at those times, because it was then that she was most aware of how much she cared. But the point is that growth occurred in both Alice and Al as they learned to deal more honestly and openly with themselves and their emotions. And this experience would have been short-circuited for both of them if divorce had been as automatically sought as it was automatically suggested.

It is not being claimed here that every affair will have salutary effects. But it is important that society take its head out of the sand long enough to be aware that extramarital affairs are not always the disasters we like to assume and that it is not unusual for marriages to be strengthened and married love to be deepened by the forces that extramarital affairs sometimes set in motion.

# XIII

# CAN RELIGION HELP?

THE QUESTION OF whether religion can help us experience and express love is not simple. Either a "Yes!" or a "No!" answer would find many outspoken adherents.

Much can be said on both sides. On one hand it seems undeniable that much of our idealism about love has had its origin and perpetuation in the Jewish and Christian traditions in our culture. In principle, at least, most of us value love and long for the satisfactions that experiencing and expressing love might bring in our personal, family, community, and national lives. The presence of this longing undoubtedly is related to our religious heritage, perhaps particularly to the New Testament and such passages as the following:

If I speak in the tongues of men and of angels, but have not love, I am a noisy gong or a clanging cymbal. And if I have prophetic powers, and understand all mysteries and all knowledge, and if I have all faith, so as to remove mountains, but have not love, I am nothing. If I give away all I have, and if I deliver my body to be burned, but have not love, I gain nothing.

And when we do achieve some degree of emotional

intimacy in what may appear to be a nonreligious or even an irreligious setting, we are probably deceiving ourselves if we disclaim the influence of our religious heritage on these experiences.

But on the other hand, the church has a rather poor record in helping people experience the love of which so much is spoken. Despite lip service to the primacy of love in human relationships, the church, by and large, tends in practice to see moral value primarily in terms of external behavior rather than in terms of the experience of love. As a result of this approach, religious groups often appear to be concerned primarily with judging people. They judge some people acceptable and stamp them with their good behavior seal of approval and make them feel welcome as long as their behavior remains acceptable. They judge others unacceptable and make them feel unwelcome, or at least uncomfortable, unless they "repent" and change their behavior to meet the group's standards.

As a result, the experience of being accepted, loved, and enjoyed as a person, irrespective of externals, is probably a rare experience in the church. And so the doors to the experience and expression of love are often rather effectively shut. And they are pushed shut under the guise of being lovingly concerned for the welfare and happiness, both present and eternal, of the individual!

## Condemning Tendencies

We have already seen how the tendencies to condemn, so prevalent in the church, are frequently incorporated into the life of "religious" families. To the child of such a family, religion often becomes a strong additional force in his feeling of rejection and his increasing hatred of himself. He is taught that he is inherently evil and that it is only through "God's gracious mercy" that he can be saved from himself. And although it is made clear to him that good behavior will not be of sufficient merit to win God's acceptance of a naturally sinful person like himself, he is nevertheless subjected to strong emphasis on various rules of conduct. It is no surprise that he feels that he is under constant surveillance by his family, his religious group, and God, and that they are all judging his worth by his actions. Feeling condemned on all sides, he attempts some form of escape from his growing self-hate. But as we have seen, such efforts lead only to further feelings of rejection.

Many people whose lives are deeply intertwined with a religious group find it difficult to experience and express love because they have a tendency to suppress or repress many of their feelings. It is within many of these groups that people are most forcefully confronted with the idea that they are committing a sin if they feel angry, covetous, jealous, or sexual in relation to others. Many churches are so condemning toward these feelings that their members are likely to avoid expressing them and may deny even to themselves that they exist. And as we have seen in the discussions of anger and sex, it is difficult to experience our love when we are full of unexpressed and unrecognized feelings that create barriers between ourselves and others.

In this context of life, as in others where we are so adept at creating barriers to love, it begins to look as though we are so frightened of love that we need the hindrances we create. No doubt it would be an oversimplification to see fear of love as the only factor in churches' apparent need to codify behavior and judge people accordingly, but it is at least one very important underlying factor.

Religious groups, like people in general, have not

understood their fear of intimacy. Without realizing it, they have encouraged emotional distance between people rather than the experience of love they professed to promote. For example, churches often substitute apparent expressions of love for the experience of intimacy. A good illustration of this exists in those thousands of congregations (not all by any means) in our society who willingly give money to missionary enterprises throughout the world, including Africa, proclaiming their "love for all mankind" but who would be very upset and uncomfortable if an American Negro braved the evident fear, suspicion, and hostility and attempted to worship with them and become active in their congregation.

In an effort to promote "fellowship" many congregations have coffee hours after church services. The typical remoteness and lack of self-revelation that usually marks these functions makes them even less productive of the experience of love than the average cocktail party, where people sometimes feel relatively free to be themselves and express some of their genuine feelings.

Churches form study groups, women's groups, men's clubs, and couples' organizations. Although these groups talk about love and fellowship, they usually speak in very rational and impersonal ways. Such groups tend to become very uncomfortable and quickly change the subject if anyone begins to express deeply personal feelings about the subject under discussion. If intimate relationships form between members of these groups, as they undoubtedly sometimes do, it is accomplished outside of the group and almost in spite of it, for there is little or nothing within it to encourage the experience of love.

During church services the minister often talks about the feeling of love and communion, which he presumes the worshipers feel with God and with each other as they worship. If he were sufficiently self-aware, it might be more helpful if the minister could tell his people that he, like them, is aware of an awful loneliness and longing for love that is almost too frightening to act upon.

Another way in which the church often promotes emotional distance is that it discourages honesty within its community. This happens because the church's preoccupation with behavior fosters the impression among its adherents that they will be condemned rather than accepted and loved if they are themselves. So the church becomes a place where people do not say things many of them often say in other life situations, "damn," "hell," "shit," etc. It becomes a place where people pretend they do not do things which they sometimes do: drink, smoke, act primarily in terms of the profit motive in their businesses, fornicate, get angry with their children—whatever their particular congregation would disapprove of. And it becomes a place where people pretend they don't feel things that they really do feel: anger, lust, prejudice, fear of love.

We all wear masks, of course, to protect us from the self-revelation that would make us feel naked and vulnerable to those around us, and we will never discard them entirely, but the atmosphere that most churches create, in which members feel they will be condemned if they say or do the "wrong" thing, makes the possibility of genuineness and the experience of love within the religious community even more difficult.

## Conversion

What happens when significant personality changes do occur within the context of our religious communities?

There is no question that remarkable changes in life occur in many individuals who pass through a crisis-type experience, which the church may call a "conversion" or simply a "religious experience." Perhaps it will be instructive to view such an experience through the eyes of Martin, a man now in his forties whose "conversion" occurred when he was in high school.

Martin was the son of a small-town minister of one of the larger Protestant denominations in America. The father was by no means a "fire and brimstone" preacher. He was, in fact, a rather warm, gentle, and shy man who lacked the aggressiveness to attract the attention of larger congregations. Though reserved, he probably expressed his affection to Martin and his other children, especially when they were small. That he loved them and took pride in them there is no doubt. There was never any severe physical punishment in the family. He was, however, much concerned that his children behave properly.

Martin recalls one incident in particular that illustrates this: "I was quite small at the time—maybe four or five. I was playing outside and was so engrossed in what I was doing that I didn't want to stop and go inside when I needed to urinate. Besides, the idea of doing it outside as Dad and I did when we were on fishing trips appealed to me. So I did it right there, which happened to be alongside the church and somewhat protected from view, so I thought. But I wasn't safe at all! Dad came along just then and spotted me. I'm sure no punishment was meted out, and I can't remember what he said, but I do remember feeling I had done a pretty terrible thing!"

Martin's mother was very affectionate, as he remembers it. She appeared to enjoy cuddling her children, and especially him. But she, too, was very concerned about matters of behavior. When he was no older than eight or nine, she extracted a promise from him that he would never smoke. The degree to which her own fears about herself were involved in her attitudes are revealed by something she said to him later as a teen-ager. At a moment when they were alone together she said, "Son, you and I are very sensitive people. We don't go in for things halfway. If you or I ever took a drink of alcohol, we would probably end up alcoholics."

When he was around twelve, the question of church membership arose. Martin's parents did not tell him he had to join. They simply told him he was old enough to join if he wanted to. He felt, however, that there was an expectation on their part and the congregation's part that the minister's son would become a church member. Yet he had many doubts and questions. He was not sure that God existed; and furthermore he was aware of anger and resentment that he did not think Christians should feel. Furthermore, he was becoming more and more aware of sexual feelings, which were at the same time exciting and frightening. These, too, he felt were feelings that a Christian should not have. He felt very guilty about these doubts and feelings, but unfortunately he did not feel free to discuss them with his parents or anyone else. So he joined the church and felt guilty about that, too!

Four or five years later his father became the minister of a struggling neighborhood church. The church was torn by internal struggles and the father, probably in an effort to unify the congregation, agreed to suggestions by the more conservative members that an evangelist be engaged. For Martin it was an emotional week of nightly meetings. The music was joyful and contagious, but he could enter in only half-heartedly, burdened down by the "knowledge" that he was not really a Christian. He wanted desperately to confess his hypocrisy, but could not bring himself to do so. On the final evening of meeting and during the last call for those who "want to accept the Lord Jesus as their personal Savior" to hold up their hands "while every head is bowed," he held up his hand.

Relief was not immediate. He went home and spent a restless night. The next morning, a Sunday, he sought out the evangelist at church and asked to speak to him. They went to a private room where he told the evangelist of his doubts and his feeling of sin. They prayed together, and the evangelist assured him of God's love and desire to forgive him. It was then that Martin suddenly felt loved and accepted. A great sense of being right with God and mankind swept over him. He felt twelve feet high and the world suddenly seemed a wonderful place in which to be alive! He really felt like he was, as the evangelist might have put it, "a new man in Christ Jesus."

The congregation soon became aware of what had happened. And although Martin's mother at first expressed some bewilderment that such an experience should have been necessary, family and congregation expressed their delight and approval at his new and wonderful awareness of the Christian faith. And Martin himself was filled with feelings of good will and love for all mankind.

From a psychological standpoint, it would appear that this experience in Martin's life could be described as an interruption in the rejection cycle. Having been filled with feelings of self-hate, guilt, and self-condemnation, he suddenly felt worthwhile and loved by God and the Christian community. He felt "cleansed of sin," and "born again," no longer an object of self-hatred but a "son of God by adoption."

Had he at the time been able to put his beliefs into words, Martin might have said something like this: "I now know that God loves me and forgives me for having been and for being the terrible person that I am. Therefore, I am released from the terrible burden of self-hate and guilt that has plagued me and am free to be more creative and more loving."

In terms of the rejection cycle, what happened might look like this:

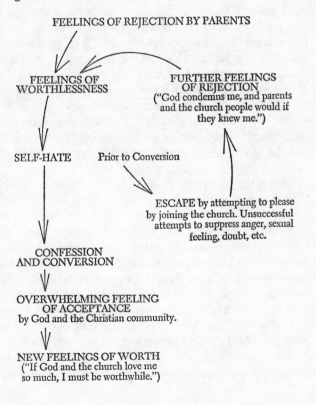

FEELINGS OF REJECTION BY PARENTS

FEELINGS OF WORTHLESSNESS

FURTHER FEELINGS OF REJECTION ("God condemns me, and parents and the church people would if they knew me.")

SELF-HATE

Prior to Conversion

ESCAPE by attempting to please by joining the church. Unsuccessful attempts to suppress anger, sexual feeling, doubt, etc.

CONFESSION AND CONVERSION

OVERWHELMING FEELING OF ACCEPTANCE by God and the Christian community.

NEW FEELINGS OF WORTH ("If God and the church love me so much, I must be worthwhile.")

There is no denying that a remarkable change occurred in Martin's life. Change in behavior may not have been particularly noticeable, since he had always done pretty much what had been expected of him. But one cannot listen to him describe the experience without being aware that a dramatic change did occur in his feeling of being condemned by God, a change that had a significant effect on many of his attitudes.

Many members of religious communities live out their lives at this level of understanding whether they reach it by a "conversion" experience, as Martin did, or by a gradual growth process in a religious home. And many people seem relatively happy in this life. It costs them something in spontaneity, for they go to considerable psychological effort to keep many of their feelings suppressed. And when they slip back and do things they "should not" do, say things they "should not" say, or feel things they "should not" feel, they again feel guilty, confess, and feel forgiven again for their "sins." They rejoice in the amount of love they feel for others, although the sensitive outsider may feel they are more condemning than loving.

The catch in Martin's adjustment to his kind of religious community is that it is based on a view that regards man as inherently evil. And Martin's "conversion" bears much resemblance to the escape hatch in which the person tries to escape feelings of self-hate by attempts to please. By saying in effect, "I have been an unworthy sinner who should be condemned, but I intend henceforth to lead a life of faith and dedication to the service of God," the individual often does win a favorable response from family, the religious community, and, he believes, from God.

But the hazards that go along with attempts to please are potentially attendant here also. The individual is likely to come to feel that the love he experiences is conditional upon his performance and therefore is not really directed toward him as a person. And, too, although he may keep his feelings of self-hate largely repressed, they are potentially increased, for in becoming a convert he has given up much of his freedom to be an individual in his own right. He is dedicated to hating and eradicating feelings that are an important part of himself, particularly his anger and many of his sexual feelings. To accomplish this he becomes more repressed and less spontaneous in his behavior.

Martin eventually came to this conclusion: he entered seminary and followed his father into the ministry, but he found that he was not successful in suppressing the feelings he felt were wrong and for which he had sought forgiveness. He married while he was in college, but he found that he felt sexually attracted to women other than his wife. This was "sinful," so he felt guilty, embarrassed, and inept around women. There were many times when he felt depressed or sullen toward other people and helpless to do anything about it, for to be aware of anger would be a sin in itself. To express it directly would be unthinkable. He also found himself tending to be critical and condemning people for doing things he later realized were things he wanted to do but did not feel free to do.

Eventually Martin found his way into a therapeutic program where he discovered he could be loved for himself as a person—not for what he pretended to be. In this "secular" setting what might be described as an even more basic "conversion" occurred. In a process that will be described more fully later, he experienced much more fundamental feelings of self-worth than he had ever experienced before.

Was Martin's religious conversion as a high school boy a negative experience in his life? He does not feel that it was. He says, "Although I no longer accept the view of man or God on which that experience was founded, nevertheless it was a turning point in my life. At a time when I needed it most, it gave me a feeling of being worth something, however shaky that feeling may have proved later. It's certainly not the route to self-acceptance that I would choose for others to follow. But for me, at that time and in that environment, it may well have been the only way that held any hope for me." So for Martin it might be fair to say that religion was both a hindrance and a help.

## What Kind of Religion?

Perhaps the central question of this chapter should not be "Can religion help?" but rather, "What kind of religion can help?" What type of religious belief and what kind of community of believers would be consistently helpful in a thoroughgoing way in aiding people to experience love?"

The God of such a faith would love each of us unconditionally in the sense that nothing that we could do would destroy that love. If we ascribe other humanlike emotions to him, we might envision him becoming angry, hurt, or sad about what we do; but the basic underlying love would be constant. He would not be interested in punishing us, instead his focus of attention would be on loving us and being loved by us. He would, of course, be concerned for our welfare and happiness. God would see existence clearly. The fact that we develop very destructive ways of dealing with each other would not be hidden or glossed over by him. He would not condemn us for the awful messes we get ourselves into, but would understand that they occur because of our self-hate and our fear of being hurt if we allow ourselves to show that we love and desire love in return.

The religious community would exemplify these same attitudes toward themselves, each other, and those outside the community insofar as humanly possible. They would recognize that they, too, are caught in the same dilemmas as all of mankind and would acknowledge the fear of love within themselves, which would limit their freedom to be loving. They would be concerned primarily with creating a climate in which people could experience the love and acceptance that would break through self-hate, thereby freeing them to experience and express love.

It would be likely that these experiences would take place most effectively in small, potentially intimate groups. In these groups honesty and genuineness would be the keynote. When individuals felt angry with each other, they would be encouraged to express their anger in whatever words might seem most appropriate without concern about whether they were "proper" or not. They would be encouraged to experience and express all their feelings: anger, hurt, jealousy, whatever. And out of it all might come a feeling of their mutuality as human beings and the awareness that they do not need to hide from each other and experience only some pale substitute for love. They might discover the intense sense of loving and being loved for which we long but which is so frightening to us.

Does such a God exist? This is a question each person must decide for himself. It is a matter of faith. Perhaps it is not so far removed as we may imagine from the God Jesus followed, if the encrustations of centuries of legalizing tendencies of the church can be scraped away. Apparently some Christian leaders feel this way, for they have moved in the direction of such a faith.

Can such a religious community exist? It remains a question whether such honesty could be tolerated within the established churches. Some movement in that direction has taken place, but it is scattered and meets with opposition. But if the church is to retain any relevance whatsoever to life, something of the sort must occur. Perhaps some appropriation of ideas from other faiths or other ways of life could infuse new life. Or perhaps religion must find a new life outside the organized church with new beginnings by those who are able to see and dare to try that which the established church could not tolerate.

# XIV

# TOWARD HEALTHY FAMILIES

ALMOST ALL OF US who are involved in families desire to create a family environment in which each member will grow in the ability to experience and express love. We want our children to learn how to love. We want them to develop a minimum of the fear of love that would cripple them in their ability to establish increasingly deep and meaningful relationships as they grow to maturity. We want them in adulthood to be able to look back at their homes as places where they felt secure and loved and at the same time felt encouraged to plunge into the mainstream of life.

We are not particularly confused about what we want in our family life. We are, however, very likely confused about how to accomplish what we want. One of the reasons for our confusion is that we parents often tend to think in terms of techniques, a tendency that is encouraged by many writings on the rearing of children. We feel if we can just find the "right" way of handling situations as they arise in the family and avoid the "wrong" ways, we will be successful.

## Quality Counts

Family life is much more complex (and in some ways perhaps more deceptively simple) than that. If it were totally a matter of right and wrong techniques, these skills would long ago have been scientifically ferreted out, written down, and we could all be successful "cookbook parents," measuring out just the right amounts of the appropriate reactions to our children. But the *quality* of our family relationships counts much more than the techniques we use. And while it is certainly true that many worthwhile things can be, and have been, said about particular ways of handling family problems, it is also true that parents who are full of fears often subtly adapt the "best" techniques in the direction of unhealthy results.

"Family councils" not infrequently provide an example of this. The council is formed for the expressed purpose of allowing the total family to have a voice in decisions that effect all the members. Very often the democratic nature of such councils is more apparent than real. The parents may in reality be afraid to turn any genuine decision-making power over to the children and yet at the same time they are uncomfortable with making arbitrary decisions. So they "kid themselves" into thinking they are being democratic by seeming to give the children a voice in family affairs while they subtly manipulate the family into doing what they wanted all along. If the children are fooled at all by this sham democracy, so much the worse. It would certainly be more honest and much less confusing to the children if parents simply announced their decisions and dealt directly with any protests that arose; yet a *genuinely* democratic family council might be a great thing.

Another technique that may be good in theory but which is often abused is the idea that parents ought to be permissive in allowing the child a great deal of freedom and a wide range of activities unhindered by adult interruption. It is not unusual for parents who are afraid of deep emotional involvement to use this approach as a subtle excuse to withdraw from their children. Probably without being fully aware of what they are doing, they develop a relationship that to the children must appear to be one of disinterest and lack of concern.

When Martha takes four-year-old son, Jamie, to visit the neighbor and Jamie starts jumping up and down on the neighbor's best sofa, Martha may be angry but may say nothing for fear of wounding the little tyke's delicate ego! But by keeping quiet Martha will not only lose her welcome at her neighbor's, she will also deprive Jamie of her genuine response. It is that honest reaction that will be most helpful to Jamie's ego, even if it is given forcibly on the seat of his pants!

So the quality of our parenthood depends not so much on our skills but rather on our maturity and our emotional openness and freedom to be real people to our children. And this, of course, depends upon the total fabric of our life and experience. And improvement as parents will come not so much through acquiring new skills as in gaining a deeper understanding and acceptance of ourselves.

## Parents' Fears

It may help, for example, if we can become aware of and accept the fact that as parents we are frightened. One reason we are afraid is that we live in rapidly changing times. We may feel the changes are for the better or for the worse, or, more likely, we will feel that some of the change represents improvement while some represents backward steps. But in any case we are frightened, because changes from old patterns of life in which we felt relatively secure and comfortable are always frightening.

This is not new, of course. Every generation has its tensions with the preceding and succeeding generations. But the rapidity of technological change in these days probably increases the problem. We who grew up without television, for example, are frightened about the effect of this instrument on the lives of our children. We may feel that there are ways in which it is potentially harmful, and we may feel guilty that we are not doing more about it, and yet we do not know just what to do. We are confused and frightened.

Another reason we are likely to be frightened as parents is that we are afraid our children are like us and have the same feelings and desires within themselves that we find unacceptable in ourselves. So if we have not learned to accept anger within ourselves, our fear may lead us to squelch our children's expression of anger even when it may be natural and appropriate.

Sexual curiosity of our children often meets a similar fate. Almost none of us are completely comfortable with our sexual feelings. We are afraid of our own sexual desires, so we are afraid of the sexual desire that we assume our children have or will develop, with the result that when our child asks where babies come from we cannot be easily direct, honest, and matter-of-fact as we could if they asked where bread comes from. We talk easily with them about eye, ear, nose, and throat, as though we were a medical specialist in them. Arms and legs pose no problem, nor does seeing, hearing, smelling, or running, but penis, vagina, and sexual intercourse are most difficult for us to say. Sometimes we parents feel these words are too difficult for our children to say or understand. But the difficulty is ours, not theirs. If you think this is not so, bring home some pumpernickel and tell the four-year-old what he is eating and see how quickly and with what delight he learns to say it! It is interesting to note in passing that there is no shortage of vivid, short, four-letter words of historic Anglo-Saxon origin for sexual and eliminative organs and functions. Unfortunately these have become "dirty" words and inappropriate for polite usage, which emphasizes how deep-seated and long-standing our sickness as a culture is in our hatred and mistrust of our sexual feelings.

In all probability we are also frightened that our children will not accept us as we are. Many words are written, including many in this book, about children's feelings of rejection by their parents. Little is said about our feelings that we may not be accepted by our children. And yet this fear is probably a strong force operating in parent-child relationships. As parents we often wear masks that prevent our children from seeing us as we really are. Often it becomes increasingly difficult as the children grow older for us to be open and genuine with them. For example, many young adults report that it is almost impossible for them to imagine their parents having sexual intercourse, although as they say, "It must have happened, since I am here!" The most important reason for this is probably that the parents tended to conceal from their children their affection for each other and particularly their sexual interest in each other.

For us as parents, as in our other relationships, our most basic fear is probably our fear of love and the vulnerability that love involves. We have discovered through many experiences that it is risky to love deeply and openly, and we find ways of withdrawing from our children.

One mother in her twenties whose children are still

under school age says, "I find myself holding back some of my feelings of love for my children. I don't want them to become too important to me. All around me I see children growing up and leaving their parents alone with nobody to care about them. I don't want that to happen to me." So her conscious resolution to this problem of eventual separation is to cheat herself out of eighteen to twenty years of the enjoyment of love so that the shock of parting will be cushioned by her studied indifference!

Although most of us are not so aware of needing to withdraw, we probably find many ways to avoid simply relaxing and enjoying our "kids" just as they are here and now. We pick and nag about relatively unimportant bits of behavior, or we become so preoccupied with their future and their scholastic achievement that we continually hound them. It is likely that it all stems from our fear of letting ourselves and them know how much we really care for them and how vulnerable our love makes us.

## Enjoying Our Children

In our discussion up to now we have taken some long, hard looks at the negative aspects of family relationships and their effects on our children's lives. We might almost despair of the possibility of having healthy families. And it *is* important to recognize that these emotionally damaging qualities are and always will be to some extent present in our families, for we are all caught up in the dilemma of our human imperfections. But the picture is not totally black by any means. Children do grow up in our families learning something about how to experience and express love, and the degree to which this occurs is not immutably fixed. It is possible to become more effective in our ability to love in spite of our fear and also possible to help our children become loving.

The New Testament contains a profound psychological insight into the process by which children learn to love. The words are: "We love, because He first loved us." (I John 4:19) The "He" implies that God is the first cause of love. The psychological impact becomes clear if we rephrase the sentence to read: "We love, because we first experienced love." And whether faith leads us to attribute the origin of love to God or not, we can agree that our *experience* of love comes to us through the imperfect channel of other persons. And the most significant persons for children are usually parents.

This experience of learning to love by being loved is much more profound than simply seeing and imitating the behavior of loving persons. It has much more to do with the child's emerging ideas and feelings about himself, which tend either to free him or inhibit him in his ability to experience and express love.

In the discussion of the rejection cycle it was emphasized that all people experience feelings of rejection that lead to feelings of worthlessness and self-hate. The experience varies greatly in the degree of feelings of rejection, but it is universal.

## The Cycle of Acceptance

Now, as we look at the positive side of the picture, it can be shown that a cycle of acceptance is taking place in children's lives during the same years the rejection cycle is establishing personality difficulty. The acceptance cycle, too, is a universal experience. Again it is a matter of degree.

The acceptance cycle begins with the child's earliest experiences of love and acceptance. This process, too, begins long before the child can form thoughts. In fact it probably begins within the first few hours of life. The sensation of touch plays a very important role. The gentle, loving, stroking touches of the mother when she is enjoying the baby are undoubtedly enjoyable to the baby. And when the infant, as it nurses from the breast or the bottle, is cuddled and cooed over, the physical and emotional warmth communicates itself.

When these experiences are contrasted with those that sometimes occur when the woman is very frightened of emotional closeness, it becomes very apparent that even these early experiences tend toward a sense of acceptance or rejection. Consider the effect on the child, for example, of the mother who is in strong conflict about her feminine role, who forces herself to breast-feed her child because she feels she should do so, although doing it makes her very angry or disgusted because of her conflicting feelings about it. Her feelings are certain to be reflected in the way she handles the child. Or another woman may be so frightened of the emotional involvement that she cannot permit herself to satisfy her own desires to cuddle the child. So she tends to withdraw and handle the child as little as possible. Still another woman may have a great deal of psychological conflict with eliminative functions and communicate her disgust in the way she changes and cleans the baby.

As the child grows older the avenues by which he senses acceptance and love (or rejection) from his parents become more numerous and more subtle. He feels acceptance when parents enjoy him, trust him, listen to him, respond to him as a person, and encourage him to accept increasing responsibility for himself without pushing him.

The sense of touch remains important. And sometimes it becomes more difficult. Some parents who found it relatively easy to enjoy expressing physical affection to their babies find themselves becoming less spontaneously affectionate to them as they grow older. The most important reason for this is probably the growing sense of vulnerability. The risk of being hurt by a baby seems rather remote, apart from the chance of death or catastrophic illness. But as the child grows older and is able to say "I hate you!" or "You're a bad mother!" or "I don't think you love me as much as Billy's father does!" we are put on notice in a multitude of ways that the "age of innocence" is past and that the possibility of emotional hurt is ever present. It is then that physical affection may not seem as natural.

One mother, Evelyn, has what might be described as a "rough-housing relationship" with her pre-teen-age children. It is difficult for her to express affection directly in hugging them. It is easy for her to pinch and jostle them until she sometimes ends up in an all-out wrestling match with them. Like other forms of teasing, these bouts are probably a relatively safe way of expressing affection. Because of her fears of being hurt and rejected by anyone to whom she feels close, Evelyn finds this type of physical contact with her children more comfortable. She satisfies some of her need for physical closeness without saying directly "I love you." And while it would be helpful if Evelyn were more free to express affection directly, even the tussling probably communicates some acceptance to the children and some of her desire to be involved with them. It may well provide a means for both Evelyn and her children to express some of their resentments, too.

To the degree that the child experiences the security of parents who are able to communicate their love and acceptance in a relatively open and direct manner, he is likely to react with positive feelings toward himself. The emotional logic of the child must be something like this: "These people who are so significant in my life love me and consider me to be of value. Therefore I must be worthwhile."

## The Child's Self-acceptance

Out of this awareness of value as a person, the child develops feelings of self-acceptance, just as feelings of self-hate tend to grow out of feelings of worthlessness. As a matter of fact, the term "love of one's self" is entirely appropriate in describing these attitudes of self-acceptance, if we can strip away all the unfortunate connotations that have been mistakenly associated with the idea of "self-love."

One of the effects of the child's feeling of worth and the resulting self-acceptance is that he will not have the need to deny feelings within himself. There will be a tendency to have an operational feeling, which, if it could be put into words, might go something like this: "Since I am a person of worth, I am not suddenly 'bad' or 'dirty' if I become aware of feelings of anger or sexual feelings. They are part of me too."

When the child does not expend his emotional resources attempting to suppress and repress "unacceptable" feelings, then he is freed to discover ways to use and enjoy his emotional responses to people. Thus a child can learn that he can express his anger when others try to take advantage of him and that he does not have to let people walk over him. He can also learn that it is ultimately destructive to himself if in his anger he becomes destructive toward others or their property.

Again, it is well to remind ourselves that we are speaking in relative terms. Everyone experiences some feelings of rejection, and thus some feelings of self-hate. But the person who is fortunate enough to have had parents who were largely accepting in their attitudes is likely to become relatively self-accepting. And this person will have relatively little need to escape from feelings of self-hate. He will not, for example, have to be falsely confident about himself. He will be able to be realistic about himself, accepting the fact that he is not, and need not be, perfect, so he will not have to be constantly on the defensive. Such a child will tend to be open and genuine in his relationships with other people. Because of this openness he will generally meet with favorable responses from others, and since he has been relatively emotionally honest, he will not be likely to mistrust these favorable reactions because he will not feel that he has "seduced" others into liking him.

These generally favorable responses the child experiences begin with the family and spread out in ever-widening circles as he encounters more and more people in his adventuring into the world. And each such favorable response reinforces his feelings of worth and self-acceptance. Thus a cycle of acceptance occurs.

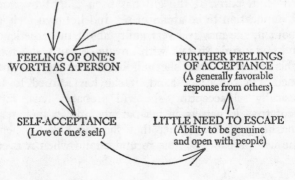

FEELINGS OF ACCEPTANCE BY PARENTS

FEELING OF ONE'S WORTH AS A PERSON

FURTHER FEELINGS OF ACCEPTANCE (A generally favorable response from others)

SELF-ACCEPTANCE (Love of one's self)

LITTLE NEED TO ESCAPE (Ability to be genuine and open with people)

It is inevitable, of course, that the growing child will not always receive accepting responses as he makes his creative thrusts into the world around him. He will encounter people who are incapable of accepting others. He will probably, for example, have at least one emotionally unhealthy teacher during his early school years. He will meet people who will criticize him, some who will treat him unjustly, some who will bully him. But when he encounters these inevitable sporadic rebuffs and hurts he will have sufficient self-acceptance and confidence that his general sense of well-being as a person will not be shattered. And he will be more able than a less self-accepting child to deal realistically with situations that arise. If, for example, a teacher criticizes his work, he will be less apt to take it as a complete damning of himself as a person. And since he does not have to see himself as perfect, he can afford to listen to the teacher's comments and profit from them if they seem valid or ignore them if they seem unimportant or incorrect.

Even the severe traumas that we would hope our children might be spared will be far less damaging if they should occur. Suppose, for example, that a seven-year-old girl is sexually molested but physically unharmed by an adult man who escapes unnoticed by any third party. If the girl has been taught by word or implication to be afraid of sex and her own feelings about it, she may feel very guilty about the experience and yet unable to talk with anyone because she feels ashamed and thinks she will be condemned or punished. On the other hand, if she has learned to be basically self-accepting, she will probably have sufficient trust in herself, in her parents, and in their relationship with each other that she can talk to them. She will probably be able to understand when it is explained to her that the man who accosted her has problems that caused him to approach her as he did. So the experience will probably not cause her to have any permanent reaction against men in general or against sex. She has too good a foundation of acceptance of herself and her feelings.

It is worth noticing that the cycle of acceptance is also the process, described earlier, by which a child moves from dependency toward increasing independence, which in turn makes deeply meaningful relationships more possible. One aspect of this is particularly relevant here. As the child becomes more and more self-accepting as a result of his experiences of feeling accepted, he becomes less and less dependent on the responses of others as a measure of his self-worth. He becomes increasingly able to stand on his own feet, think his own thoughts, and act in self-affirming ways without the likelihood that disapproval or discouragement will shatter his feeling of self-worth.

While the effort is being made to avoid the hazards of outlining techniques of child-rearing, it may nevertheless be helpful to attempt to state some general principles about family life that are corollary to the cycle of acceptance.

## Parents' Bill of Rights

For one thing, it needs to be kept clearly in focus that parents are people, too! One of the problems inherent in talking about the importance of acceptance in family relationships is that parents are likely to demand of themselves that they be accepting 100 per cent of the time, whether they feel like it or not, and that they are likely to define acceptance as meaning that the parent should never become angry, never "put his foot down," never express a contrary opinion, and in general should become a nonentity in relation with his children.

When this happens, the parent has become a second-class citizen in the home, one who encourages his children in the free expression of feeling but denies himself the same right, for the fact is that we do not always feel accepting of our children. Sometimes the "little darlings" seem more like "monsters." For parents to try to appear "accepting" when they feel angry is to be phony and in reality to be unaccepting, for it betrays a lack of trust in the child to deal with us as we really are.

It is quite possible for us to be very open with our children about our opinions and our feelings without demanding that they agree with us and without attempting to control their behavior. One mother became very concerned about the clothes her daughter was wearing to high school. To her mind the girl was coming up with "goofy combinations." In discussing the matter with a friend, she said, "Those getups she wears really bug me, but I don't say anything about them because I think it's important for her to be able to make her own decisions about these things. I know if I had dressed like that when I was in high school, my mother would have said, 'Get those clothes off and put these on this moment!' And I just don't feel like I want to boss my daughter around that way." Apparently it had never occurred to her that she could express her feelings and opinions about her daughter's clothing without robbing the girl of her right to make her own decisions, so she was adopting an attitude of studied indifference that might have given the girl the false impression that her mother had no interest or concern about her appearance.

It is far better to be sufficiently self-accepting of our

feelings as parents to be genuine with our children than it is to "work at" being "accepting" at the cost of suppressing our feelings. Our anger, hurt, or fear will be expressed indirectly in some way if we do not deal with it directly.

## What Is "Respect"?

Another general principle of family life is that it is desirable for disciplinary measures to be reserved for things that have been done and not be used for things that have been said. Many parents express a concern about "respect" at this point, saying, "If we let our children say anything they please to us, they won't have any respect for us." But when this thought is examined, the idea of forcing our children to be dishonest with us by disciplinary means seems a rather strange way to help our children consider us "worthy of high regard," to quote a Webster definition of respect.

There are too many instances of quiet, studious, industrious, and "respectful" young men or women who have spent many years bottling up anger and other feelings and who at a crisis point in their lives take up a weapon and begin slaughtering those around them to place a very high value on "respect" won this way. Fortunate indeed is the child who has learned through experience that he can tell his parents how he really feels without living in fear of retribution. And he is fortunate, too, if he has learned that he can trust them to be as honest with him. Out of this kind of relationship will grow the genuine mutual respect and love that can last a lifetime.

A quality of relaxed good humor seems to accompany the disciplinary efforts of many successful parents. For such parents the children's infractions of the

rules and the punishment meted out does not become
the deadly serious business that it does in many house-
holds. It is likely that the quality in the parents that
makes this attitude possible is their own self-acceptance. They do not feel that their worth as persons or
as parents is threatened when the child goes against
the rules, so they do something that will help the child
remember in the future. They do not feel like "bad
parents," and so they do not give the child the feeling
that he must be the "bad seed." Imagine, for example, how Martin's father, if *he* had been relaxed about
it, could have laughed, even with a five-year-old, when
he found him urinating against the church. And still
he could have gotten the message across that it would
be wise to be more discreet in the selection of a site
for the sake of the shockable ladies who might be
watching.

The relaxed good humor being described does not,
of course, include hostile ridicule and sarcasm, which
are very destructive to children. There would be little
humor and nothing salutary, for example, in the comment of a father who would say to his son in front of
the boy's friends, "You'd have remembered to take the
trash out this morning if you had more between your
ears than a jackass."

## Underrating Our Children

One factor that seems to underlie a great many problems in families is the tendency of parents to underrate
children's abilities in the area of relationships. Perhaps
we use the idea that "they couldn't possibly understand" as another device to maintain some emotional
distance between ourselves and them because of our
fear of love and its risks. In any case, *our children are
more perceptive than we think they are.* We fool them

much less than we think we do when we attempt to conceal emotions from them. When we resent them, for example, and try to hide our resentment from them, we show it in some more subtle way and they get the message. And the subtlety makes it much more difficult for them to handle than our anger.

*Our children are also much tougher than we think they are, and they can handle our negative feelings better than we think they can.* Children do not need to be handled with kid gloves. We can make a lot of mistakes in our dealings with them and they can survive quite well, particularly if we do not have to pretend that we are perfect. If we can have a genuine relationship with them in which we are not too frightened to express our love, our anger, and our other feelings, and if we can admit it when we make mistakes, they will understand, accept, and feel secure because it will have the ring of reality; because they will know that they, too, have the same feelings.

*Our children can also understand our feelings better than we think they can.* We often assume, when we are discouraged or upset about something, that our children could not understand. And we may feel that we want to protect them from some of the problems and worries that beset us. More often than not even our younger children would understand and would feel much better if they knew what was going on and why the tension exists within the family, since they sense that something is wrong.

If, for example, a family is in financial difficulties, there is likely to be a charged atmosphere throughout the home no matter how hard the parents try to conceal the facts from the children. If the children are not told what is going on, they can only guess about the cause of the tension. Their guesses will most likely be that something is wrong between family members. They may feel that the parents do not love each other any more and are going to get a divorce, as some of the other parents on the block have done. Or they may even imagine that they have done something to create all the tension that nobody wants to talk about. They will understand much better than we think they can if we will simply give them facts and feelings with which to work. It may even be a relief to them to discover that parents are human, too, and also have their worries and problems!

Everything that has been said here about family life points to the importance of the maturity of parents. Families will tend to be more healthy if parents are able to be emotionally honest and direct with their children and if they can express their love in deeply satisfying ways despite the risks of being hurt that such love always involves.

But parents, too, have been reared in families. And they, like everyone else, have been hurt in the past and have in varying degrees been emotionally crippled in their ability to accept themselves and in their freedom to express love, so the tendency exists for parents to react to their children in ways that perpetuate the fear of love from one generation to the next. Is there any escape from this social "inheritance"? Fortunately, it is possible for individuals, whether they are parents or not, who long for more satisfying experiences of love to gain more self-acceptance and self-awareness. It is a matter of learning to value ourselves.

# XV

# LEARNING TO LOVE OURSELVES

ONE OF THE MOST insulting things a person can say about another in our culture without using profanity is "Man, that guy really loves himself!" It is interesting that so many of us from very different kinds of background and having various levels of sophistication consider love of self to be a condemnable quality. In Christian circles, for example, much is said or written about "the corrupted and sinful nature of man showing forth in his acts of self-love." So strong has this tendency been within the Christian church that if an individual church member were asked what the most basic or central problem of mankind is, his answer would likely include some form of the phrase "love of self." Loving one's self has not only become a sin, but *the* sin!

This view of the love of self would appear to have developed in spite of the teachings of Jesus, for when he said, "You shall love your neighbor *as yourself*," (Mark 12:31 R.S.V.) he appears to have recognized a legitimate place in life for loving ourselves in addition to loving God and others.

At this point someone might argue, "Well, what difference does it make if we use the term 'self-love' instead of 'selfishness' or 'self-centeredness'? We know what we mean by it." But more is involved than a mere loose use of words. For we are constantly exposed throughout our lives to this idea that it is wrong to love ourselves. Children are told by parents that they ought to act primarily in terms of other people's interests and not consider their own desires and their own feelings. The child finds himself unable to do this and feels guilty. He may also feel quite confused when he looks about him and sees people, including his parents, appearing to act most of the time in terms of their own self-interest.

It is important to challenge the idea that loving ourselves is wrong, because this concept is damaging to the human personality. For one thing, it leads to the glorification of self-hate. Many who were reared in the Christian faith were exposed as children to a gospel song, the words of which are sometimes changed in more recent versions. But formerly it went like this:

> Alas and did my Savior bleed?
> And did my sovereign die?
> Would he devote that sacred head
> For such a worm as I?

To have people sing about themselves as "worms" would certainly appear to be an encouragement to them to hate themselves. Yet it would hardly seem to be an accurate description of the religion of Jesus, who was accused (and correctly!) of being a friend of the greatly despised "tax collectors and sinners."

We have already examined the damage that self-hate does to the human personality and the deteriorating effect that it has on our relationships with each other. The implication that we ought not to love ourselves but ought rather to hate ourselves does us the disservice of tending to perpetuate self-hate, our most basic neurosis.

One of the problems arising from the glorification of self-hate is that it often leads to morbid and unproductive feelings of guilt. Particularly in religious settings this often becomes so pervasive a feeling that an individual will describe himself as "feeling guilty about everything I do." Such nonspecific feeling of guilt would appear to serve no other purpose than to rob the individual of the freedom to enjoy life.

We have already seen that symptoms of personality disturbances such as bragging and bullying are not evidence that the person thinks too highly of himself, but rather that he hates himself. The same is true of the person who has qualities that cause us to describe him as selfish or self-centered. Selfishness does not result from love of self; it is self-hate masquerading as self-love, for the selfish person is very insecure on the deeper levels of his personality. He is not "in love with himself." He has never experienced his worth; because of his insecurity he must center all his life and interests about himself. He *must* be selfish. Everything *must* turn to his own advantage to protect himself from the nagging haunting suspicion that he is worthless. He is like the miser who clings to every cent, not because he gets a healthy satisfaction from his skill in earning his living, but because he has an overwhelming distrust of the future and of his ability to provide. And just as the miser cannot enjoy his money and the things it could provide, the selfish person cannot fully enjoy human relationships because of his lack of trust in himself.

Another damaging aspect of self-hate is that it often prevents us from realistic appraisals of ourselves that could lead to growth and maturity. When we hate ourselves, we become reluctant to look closely at ourselves because we cannot tolerate what we see. So instead we tend to build false images of ourselves, often based on some pseudoconfidence. As we develop these shaky images of ourselves, built on the flimsiest of foundations, we have to build strong defenses against seeing how empty and meaningless they really are. We bitterly resent and reject any criticism or apparent criticism that appears to threaten our house of cards. We do not allow ourselves to see things about ourselves that we might want to change if we saw them clearly— things that may be painfully apparent to others.

Our attitude toward our images might be compared to the child's feeling about a blanket that has become important to his feeling of security. He drags it around with him wherever he goes. It becomes dirty and tattered and an embarrassment to his parents, but for him these deficiencies simply do not exist.

We are often in a similar, but less humorous, predicament with our self-images. We are so certain at the deeper level of our personalities that our real selves are unlovable that we show the world spurious selves to which we cling desperately lest they be tampered with and our fragile security lost. We do everything possible to conceal our self-hate from ourselves. In this way we prevent ourselves from healthy appraisal of our abilities and liabilities, which might lead to personality growth. We become our own worst enemies. And often it might be said of us, as one novelist described a character, "He was not so much a human being as a civil war." It is this war within ourselves brought on by self-hate that keeps us from realizing our potentials more fully.

In certain circles one hears much praise of selflessness as a human motive. It is said that the ultimate in goodness is to have no concern for one's own welfare and to be concerned only for the welfare of others. It is unlikely that such indifference to the self can exist. And it is likely that the ideal exists, because we have tended to think that self-interest and the interest of others are mutually exclusive. We have been taught to say to ourselves, "If I am concerned with following my own feelings and satisfying my own desires, I will be destructive to those around me. Therefore, if I am to love another person I must suppress my own interests and be as they want me to be." If we could see that even this effort to subjugate ourselves to others is a striving to enhance ourselves and gain a feeling of self-worth, we would become more realistic about the all-important role of self-interest in our lives.

## Foundation for Loving Others

The major difficulty of our effort to live selfless lives is that we become more or less successful at it! As we try to please those around us, we become more and more fuzzy as individuals. Chameleonlike, we seem to become like those in whose presence we are at the moment. This is a basic problem of those whose lives are centered in "giving of themselves." If this is their primary motive in life, they soon have very little "self" to give. The theologian Paul Tillich once said, "It is time to end the bad theological usage of jumping with moral indignation on every word in which the syllable 'self' appears."

Love of one's self is not antagonistic to having satisfying relationships. On the contrary, *we are free to love others only as we become free to love ourselves.* From the standpoint of the emotional factors involved in interpersonal relationships it would be legitimate to rephrase Jesus' statement, "You shall love your neighbor as yourself," to read, "You cannot love your neighbor until you love yourself." For hate of one's self constantly interferes with the whole gamut of our relationships from casual acquaintances to those with whom we desire to be intimate.

For one thing, we tend to be intolerant of others when we are intolerant of ourselves. And often it is the same trait with which we have difficulty within ourselves that we cannot tolerate in others. Jealousy often involves this kind of reaction. One man, Lee, had a brief encounter with another woman near the end of his second year of marriage. He and the "other woman" had sexual intercourse on only one very unsatisfying occasion. He felt very guilty about this experience. During the succeeding years of his marriage Lee was ridden with fear that he might repeat the experience. Whenever he became aware of sexual feelings for women other than his wife, Terri, he hated himself for them and became quite frightened and distrustful of himself. At the same time he developed strong feelings of jealousy toward Terri, who was a vivacious, sometimes almost flirtatious, woman. He could not tolerate in her what he found intolerable in himself; and he built a virtual prison for her, and incidentally for himself as well. He became very upset when Terri showed any warmth or interest in their male friends and alienated a number of other couples with whom they began to associate. He became very suspicious of her, frequently "checking up" on her activities. He insisted that she spend every moment possible with him. For Terri, that "trapped feeling" in marriage was no figure of speech as long as she was willing to tolerate the unreasonable demands brought on by his own self-hate and self-mistrust.

## Oversensitivity

Another way that self-hate interferes with our enjoyment of our associations with others is that it frequently leads to our being overly sensitive and too easily hurt. When we are self-condemning we tend to read condemnation into other people's words and actions. We may become so touchy that the simplest comments by others seem to have sinister condemning undertones. On the way home from a party, a wife may say in passing, "Gee, the Joneses have a beautiful home." And the husband may feel she is condemning him "for not being man enough" to have sufficient earnings to own such a home. Or he may say, "Flora Jones sure looked great tonight, didn't she?" And her reply, "Yeah, great!" may be loaded with sarcasm because she feels he is really saying, "You look pretty ugly and sloppy compared to that Flora Jones!"

This touchiness also often causes us to generalize another's critical remark in a very limited area and make it into a wholesale condemnation of ourselves. Many a wife has reacted this way to a comment from her husband at the dinner table, such as, "This macaroni and cheese tastes a little flat. I wish you had put more seasoning in it." Wife at this point may burst into tears, jump up from the table, and shout, "Nothing I ever do is right. You really hate me, don't you?" Assuming the husband does not constantly criticize her, it can safely be said that she has read a great deal of self-condemnation into his remark.

## Being Genuine

Self-hate also gets in the way of successful relationships because we do not trust ourselves to be genuine. We develop some variety of phoniness because we assume people will not like us as we really are, since we ourselves do not. Every one of us probably has one or more acquaintances who are patently phony and are rather extreme examples of this tendency. It may, for example, be a woman who grew up in poorer surround- ings than those in which she now lives. She is insecure in the new experience and, whether she allows herself to be aware of it or not, feels her current social set could not accept her if she were natural, so she "puts on airs" and acts in ways that she feels are the way a person in her setting should act; but the performance does not come off well since it is obviously false.

While most of us are not as obviously phony as such a woman, we all have some of the tendency. One way it may express itself is in an effort to be "kind" or "helpful" when we do not really feel kindly toward a person. This is a made-to-order pitfall for those who have been raised in religious families where strong em- phasis has been placed on the individual's "obligation" to be helpful and loving. In Christian homes children become familiar with such passages as:

Love is patient and kind . . . it is not arrogant or rude. Love does not insist on its own way; it is not irritable or resentful; it does not rejoice at wrong, but rejoices in the right. Love bears all things, believes all things, hopes all things, endures all things. (I Corinthians 13:3–7 R.S.V.)

These are beautiful words from a beautiful chapter. And they describe well some of the experiences that occur when we are filled with feelings of warmth and love. They are the genuine overflow toward another when we are so full of feelings of caring that we could scarcely do otherwise than be loving.

Often we turn it around. We say to ourselves, "Kind- ness is a sign of love, so I *should* be kind, therefore I *will* be kind." So we try to be kind to those for whom we may feel considerable unexpressed irritation or resentment. We remain emotionally distant because our "kindness" is phony. Our resentment is almost sure to seep through in indirect expressions, as when, for example, we seem condescending and patronizing in our "kindness." Or perhaps we feel we *should* be patient with our children, and so we act that way when we feel more like screaming at them. They sense our anger and yet have no way of coping with it directly since it remains unexpressed. And a wall of falseness stands between us because we have not trusted ourselves to be genuine.

The self-hate that makes us afraid to be ourselves gets us into very difficult binds in our relations with others because we tend to assume that we can gain affection only through acceptable performances, since we feel no one could possibly love us just because we are who we are.

Carol grew up in a home where great emphais was placed on performance. Generally, she was made to feel that anything she did in the home as a child was inadequate and that she was rather worthless. The resulting feelings of self-hate made marriage a difficult experience for her. It was inevitable that she would assume that her husband, Dan, could not possibly love her for herself, so she constantly assumed that she would have to perform well or he would abandon her. Yet she seethed with anger, because he did not love her (so she felt) without regard to her performance.

The way in which Carol kept the house became one of the focal points of this predicament. She had some tendency to let it become quite cluttered. Whenever this happened Dan became angry. He said that since there were no children and since she was not working the least she could do was to keep a reasonably picked-up house. And since he himself was frightened and full of doubts about his own lovableness, he felt—and expressed the feeling—that when she failed to keep the house uncluttered she cared nothing at all for him.

Dan's reaction added fuel to the fire as far as the dilemma that Carol felt. Anything that she did at that point was certain to be unsatisfying to her. If, in response to his anger, she busied herself and cleaned the place up, he praised her, and yet this only increased her anger, because she would say to herself, "He expresses affection only when I perform well for him. I'm not free to do as I please because he will leave me if I do. I must dedicate my whole life to pleasing him if I want him to stay with me." If, on the other hand, she rebelled, as she often did, against the feeling of having to please him and let the house become more and more cluttered, Dan became more frustrated and angry, and she would use this to confirm her feelings of self-hate, for she could say, "You see, it's true. You only love me when I do exactly what you want me to do."

Perhaps the most damaging result of Carol's preoccupation with this bind was that she became virtually emotionally paralyzed. She became unable to know what *she* wanted, so concerned was she with what *he* wanted. She could not really tell whether it was more satisfying to *herself* to live in a cluttered or an uncluttered house. Everything she did tended to be a *reaction* to Dan, rather than the *act* of a person doing what she wanted to do. Even the suggestion by Dan that they hire somebody to come in regularly and clean up was very frightening, for she told herself, "When someone is coming in and cleaning up, he'll no longer need me. Then he'll get rid of me!" Carol had never learned to love herself, and so it was difficult for her to believe that Dan could be staying with her because he loved her and wanted her for reasons other than efficiency.

Self-hate continually gets in the way of the experience of love, and it becomes evident that learning to love ourselves is a crucial and necessary experience if we hope to grow in emotional maturity and in the capacity to experience and express love. A solid, deep-rooted sense of one's worth as a person is the foundation on which personhood can be built. On this foundation we can become independent individuals who know ourselves and thus have a self for others to discover and love since we will be more able and willing to disclose ourselves. And out of this foundation of self-acceptance comes the capacity to accept others as they are, for we will find nothing in them that we have not found and accepted in one form or another in ourselves.

## Approaching Self-caring

How can we learn to love ourselves? Perhaps we can start by admitting that it is impossible! It is not possible in the sense that we will never become completely self-accepting (not in this life anyway!). Like other values worth wanting, loving one's self is an ideal never fully realized. But moving in that direction is a fascinating and worthwhile, lifelong adventure.

It will help us to become more loving toward ourselves if we can become more self-aware. It is not possible to love someone profoundly whom you do not know, and many of us are virtually strangers to ourselves, so deadened have we become to any awareness of our deeper feelings. And since we have spent many years cutting ourselves off from awareness of hated parts of ourselves, the recovery of awareness is usually not easily accomplished. We are frightened of what we may find and resist awareness in multitudes of ways. Frequently, the help of a professional therapist is needed to help us overcome these resistances.

Often in the early stages of recovering self-awareness it will seem as though we are learning to hate ourselves, not love ourselves. This happens because one of the first things we become aware of is our hidden self-hate, which has been building up over the years and of which we have likely had only vague intimations, and feelings that have been too unacceptable for us to allow ourselves to experience come to the surface. We may begin to feel more hate than we thought it was possible for us to feel. Self-loathing, deeply experienced hurt, disgust about sex, and other frightening feelings may burst into awareness.

This is a crisis in personal growth, but it is often a necessary crisis. Advocates of positive-thinking approaches to mental health frequently do a disservice at this point. Too often they short-circuit this process by encouraging individuals to think positively about themselves without taking into account their need to first experience their self-hatred. Under the influence of this advice individuals are likely to gain a whitewash of apparent "self-acceptance" and "self-affirmation" over the tomb of their inner deadness to themselves and their self-hate. In this way they may talk themselves into being more successful insurance salesmen or less disagreeable husbands, while they have only cut themselves off even farther from contact with themselves and the ultimate possibility of genuine self-acceptance and self-affirmation.

Gradually, when we allow ourselves to experience self-hate, the crisis will pass. We discover that it is not so bad after all to have very human feelings. A young woman who has been shocked and scandalized by accounts of sexual promiscuity feels profound disgust as she becomes aware that she, too, has sexual desires that are not limited to one man. But as she begins to discover that she can trust herself and that she will not become a helpless victim of her inner desires, she finds she begins to enjoy and cherish her sexual feelings. As is usually the case, her disgust masked an unaccepted appetite.

The process of becoming self-aware will be aided if we examine our critical feelings of others and our touchiness in our relationships. We have already seen that we tend to criticize others for those qualities that are unacceptable in ourselves and are easily hurt because we read self-condemnation into the reactions of others to us. These feelings that run through our minds can provide clues that will help us experience our self-hate.

Bert was a young workhorse of a man who was considerably bugged by his father's lack of ambition. He could not understand how his father could go off for a day of fishing when he was having business difficulties and financial pressures. When the young man examined his feelings more closely, it became evident that he did not allow himself to experience his own desire to "take off" and get away from it all occasionally. He was afraid he would like it too much and become a drifter. So he drove himself constantly, not allowing himself the pleasure of relaxation. And it is not surprising that once Bert was able to experience this desire to loaf within himself, he not only moved in the direction of greater self-acceptance but was able to experience more love for his father.

It will also help us in our efforts to learn to love

ourselves if we can keep our goals realistic. Many of us make severe demands on ourselves. We think we ought to be perfect, and we think we ought to achieve that perfection immediately. When we fail to do so, as we certainly must, we are burdened with unproductive feelings of guilt and worthlessness. With this kind of perfectionist cycle operating we might easily make even the search for self-acceptance a new vehicle for feelings of worthlessness!

Perhaps the secret lies in learning to relax and enjoy what we are right now—every feeling, every urge, every idiosyncrasy that is a part of us. Then if we really *want* to be what we have always told ourselves we *ought* to be, we may be freer to move in that direction. In other words, we dare not wait until we are perfect to start loving ourselves. We would wait forever. Let us learn to love ourselves in our imperfections. This attitude toward ourselves might be compared to the attitude of a warmly affectionate father toward his son. He does not stop loving his son when the boy makes mistakes. He recognizes the failures and probably will express his concern and perhaps may even become angry. But somehow there is communication from father to son of steadfast love and encouragement that is not destroyed or even threatened by these occasional crises.

A similar attitude toward ourselves is very desirable. There will, of course, be times when we feel we have "goofed." We may be angry and say to ourselves, "Oh, you stupid ass, you've done it again." But if there is a basic underlying sense of personal worth that is not shaken by the recognition that we have made a mistake, we can be much more effective about doing what we want to do in the future; for we will not be wasting the days of our lives in self-recrimination. Often this self-accepting attitude involves a sense of humor in which we can laugh at ourselves in our errors, give ourselves a good kick in the pants, and move on to the next moment of living.

Ideally, religious faiths might play an important part in helping their believers to learn to love themselves. Perhaps they do, but frequently they tend to create self-hate. Often religion says, "You are unworthy and condemnable in God's sight. However, if you confess your unworthiness, God is willing to forgive you. You will then be a new creature, and God will give you strength to feel and act in more acceptable ways."

It cannot be denied that individuals who accept such a belief in God often experience a profound relief as they feel released from the burden of self-hate. And often they live greatly changed lives. But the question remains whether the basic problem of self-hate has been adequately dealt with or whether a veneer of self-acceptance has simply been laid over the self-condemnation. It would appear that a new and better repressive technique is often acquired whereby the individual can somewhat better avoid dealing with the desires and feelings that are still felt to be so condemnable in God's eyes.

On the other hand, religion sometimes says, "God knows how often you get into messes you regret. He also knows how ugly and brutal you can sometimes seem. But he also knows how frightened you are and understands why you do the things you do. He loves and accepts you as you are. Because he loves you he wants you to enjoy life and the experience of love to the fullest. He enjoys being a partner in your quest for that life." It seems likely that faith in this kind of God would add to the experience of love for one's self.

Our self-hate is developed primarily from experiences

of feelings of rejection by others. Learning to love ourselves also involves relationships with people. We need the experience of emotional intimacy with others so that we can learn that we can be accepted as we are and thus can grow in self-acceptance. A very real predicament faces us at this point. We are desperately afraid of intimacy because we assume that deep involvement with another person will lead only to further rejection and hurt, and further confirmation of our feelings of worthlessness and unlovableness. Yet the experience of intimacy is almost a prerequisite for moving in the direction of the greater self-acceptance that would free us to enter into intimate relationships.

The only solution to this dilemma seems to be to move gradually into increasing intimacy in spite of our fear. We will probably act somewhat like a wild deer learning to trust a would-be human friend. Because of our fear, our seeking of intimacy will undoubtedly proceed slowly and cautiously and our forward progress will include many frightened strategic withdrawals. But if we can overcome our fear sufficiently to begin to talk about our inner feelings with another human being we will begin to learn that we are not unique. And out of the mutual acceptance that we experience, a growing sense of self-acceptance will begin to assert itself. Of course such a relationship will have its difficult moments, both for ourselves and the other person, when we feel hurt, angered, misunderstood, and, above all else, frightened. This will happen because we are both so frightened of self-disclosure that we constantly seek to avoid it. If we can persist in spite of our fears, the rewards in satisfaction and growing self-acceptance will be great.

The suggestions described above for breaking through the cycle of rejection and our self-hatred and learning to love ourselves will probably be helpful if we are sufficiently motivated toward changing ourselves and if we have not been so emotionally damaged that we cannot make a start.

## Psychotherapy

Many people find their way into some form of psychotherapy or counseling as a way of interrupting the rejection cycle. They seek professional help for all kinds of reasons, of course. Some are aware, at least vaguely, of their lack of self-acceptance and how it interferes with their relationships with other people and are not content to live out their lives on that level. More often individuals find their way into psychotherapy because of some symptom of their self-hate and its corollary fear of love. They may be having marital or sexual problems, anxiety attacks, vocational problems, physical illness caused by emotional factors, or any of numerous symptoms.

What takes place in psychotherapy when it is effective in helping a person achieve a more satisfying life? This is a profoundly significant question to which many answers have been given, each involving differing theories of the human personality and its development. Although there is room for disagreement about many details of the process, one change that appears to occur in successful psychotherapy is that the person has a growing sense of his own worth as a person. And it seems likely that one of the best ways to describe the process behind this growing sense of one's value is to see it as a cycle of acceptance. The therapist working with Jane Doe in his own unique way somehow conveys to her his feeling that she is a person of worth. Jane then gradually comes to feel that she is basically accepted and respected as an individual. She begins to understand that the therapist sees through whatever annoying traits she has and the things she does that tend to destroy herself or others. She grasps that he recognizes that all of these things are symptoms of her self-hate and have nothing to do with her basic worth. She begins to sense that he cares for her.

This does not mean that the therapist remains benignly acquiescent to every reaction of the client. He may become annoyed and express his annoyance; he may become bored and express his boredom; he may feel hurt or angered by something the client says or does and express his feeling. But the very fact that he is willing to enter into the relationship this honestly and intensely, revealing his own humanness, will be an expression of trust in the client's basic ability to handle the situation. And through it all he somehow conveys the feeling, perhaps not expressed directly, that he values the client for himself and as a unique individual.

In such a relationship the client is gradually freed to be aware of more and more of his feelings that he has not allowed himself to fully experience. He becomes more free to reveal facets of himself to this accepting human being that he has hitherto revealed to no one for fear of experiencing further rejection. Gradually, with the aid of the therapist's techniques, and encouraged by the feeling of acceptance, the client discovers himself being more honest and open with himself and with the therapist. As he discovers that nothing destroys the therapist's basic attitude toward him, he begins to allow himself to have glimmerings of his own value as a person.

This is often a discouraging process. The fear of emotional intimacy is ever-present and there will be frequent setbacks as the client begins to reveal himself, becomes frightened, and withdraws into the shell of his defenses against closeness. Later, as he gives up one defense against intimacy he is likely to adopt another in its place, with little or no awareness of what he is doing.

The client is almost certain to have doubts about the genuineness of the therapist's acceptance. If these doubts remain unexpressed, they constitute a serious block to the therapeutic process. When they are expressed openly they can often be dealt with effectively. They take many forms. One person may say, "It's your job to accept me when no one else would possibly do so." Another may say, "I can't help feeling that sooner or later you will find out something about me that will cause you to have nothing more to do with me." Such ideas are very persistent because our feelings of self-hate are so persistent. One woman had been in therapy for many months and had made many gains in growing self-acceptance, which were reflected in much more satisfying relationships with people. Even so, on one occasion just before a session with her therapist, when she was feeling particularly low, she rose from her chair, from which she had been talking with a group of friends, and blurted out, "I'm going to the one person in the world who accepts me, and I *pay* him to!"

But as the client's confidence in the therapeutic relationship grows, he can begin to deal directly with his self-hate and its sources. In one therapy session, a young woman, Ellen, was making remarks that indicated she was feeling critical of herself. In order to help her experience her emotions more intensely, the therapist asked her to imagine that the "self" she was criticizing was sitting in the chair opposite her and to talk directly to that "self." She paused for a few moments, and then said, "The first thing that comes to my mind is that I want to call you a whore and a bitch, but I find I can't do that." The therapist then asked her to talk to herself about why that was difficult. She did so; and gradually as she talked it dawned on her that she did not want to call herself a "whore or a bitch" because she cared more for herself than that. Toward the end of the conversation with her "self" Ellen said with deep feeling, "I guess I really want to tell you I love you, but it seems somehow selfish." As she finished, she was crying as the relief of knowing that she could care for herself flooded over her. At the same time tears rolled down the therapist's cheeks, for he knew the same feeling from his own experience. For many moments, thereafter, Ellen and the therapist sat in silence, enjoying their sense of closeness to each other and to themselves.

As the individual in therapy gradually develops this sense of self-acceptance, he will have less need to escape into the various defenses he has used in the past. He will gain ability to be more open and self-revealing to the therapist as another human being who consistently cares for him regardless of whatever emotional interchanges they may experience together. Sometimes he will become very frightened, but gradually the awareness of the satisfactions of being one's self will be so rewarding and so productive of growing feelings of self-worth that former patterns of living will seem too unrewarding to continue.

No attempt is being made here to explain every movement in the direction of emotional health that can occur in psychotherapy. It is being suggested that perhaps the most important thing that can happen is that the cycle of rejection in the client's life is broken and a cycle of acceptance is begun. This process can be diagramed as follows:

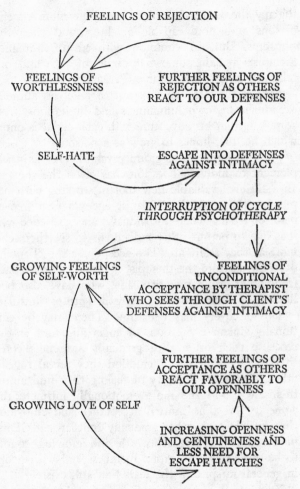

FEELINGS OF REJECTION

FEELINGS OF
WORTHLESSNESS

FURTHER FEELINGS OF
REJECTION AS OTHERS
REACT TO OUR DEFENSES

SELF-HATE

ESCAPE INTO DEFENSES
AGAINST INTIMACY

INTERRUPTION OF CYCLE
THROUGH PSYCHOTHERAPY

GROWING FEELINGS
OF SELF-WORTH

FEELINGS OF
UNCONDITIONAL
ACCEPTANCE BY THERAPIST
WHO SEES THROUGH CLIENT'S
DEFENSES AGAINST INTIMACY

FURTHER FEELINGS OF
ACCEPTANCE AS OTHERS
REACT FAVORABLY TO
OUR OPENNESS

GROWING LOVE OF SELF

INCREASING OPENNESS
AND GENUINENESS AND
LESS NEED FOR
ESCAPE HATCHES

Not every therapist, of course, is equal in the ability
to be authentic and genuinely accepting in relationship with clients. Therapists are human, too, and inevitably have experienced some degree of rejection and
self-hate. Most of them have at one time been in

therapy themselves in order to become more effective persons and more capable of direct and open relationships. But, in common with all of humanity, therapists remain somewhat afraid of love and only relatively able to be genuine. Perhaps it is likely to be a mark of the effective therapist that he can afford to experience his own humanness and limitations, freely admitting that his adventure with each client is one in which he, too, hopes to grow as a person.

The development of group psychotherapy as a supplement to individual sessions has given the therapist an additional valuable new tool in working with people. In the group the therapist encourages a free climate of feeling where individuals can experience what it is like to permit other individuals to see themselves more as they really are. The acceptance the client has experienced from the therapist is found to be available from other group members, too, who have also been limited by their fears in their experience of intimacy.

This discovery may take time. There may be emotionally violent expressions of anger and hurt as they react to each other. But gradually awareness comes that the more depth of emotion they reveal to each other, the more similarity of feeling they find among themselves, and the more emotionally intimate they come to feel. The mutual acceptance and enjoyment they find in each other gradually translates itself into increased feelings of self-worth and growing courage to be one's self with group members and with people in general in spite of the fears that still exist.

# XVI

## LIVING SPONTANEOUSLY

MANY OF US do not even allow ourselves to imagine what it would be like to feel free in our daily lives and in our interactions with other people. We are so accustomed to believing that there are certain things we "just have to do" to survive and get along reasonably well with people that we have only the vaguest notion of what it would mean to live a self-chosen or spontaneous life. We tend to make a way of life out of feeling trapped.

Perhaps we need first of all, then, to take a good look at ourselves and discover that we are kidding ourselves about not being free. We are not trapped. We almost invariably have alternative courses of action, much as we may try to persuade ourselves otherwise. We do things that we do because we choose to do them. And if we feel trapped, it is because we have chosen to feel that way for our own inner reasons. Perhaps the awareness that we have much more freedom than we choose to think we have is too frightening for us to face.

### Freer Than We Think

A considerable change might occur in our attitudes and feelings if we could grasp, not only intellectually but emotionally, the fact of our freedom. Then we would recognize that we are making choices constantly as to what we do each moment even though we often do not allow ourselves to be aware of those decisions.

Marge Smith, housewife and mother of three young children, after three rainy days of having the children in the house and underfoot continuously thinks to herself, "If I have to stay cooped up with these kids one more hour, I think I'll go out of my mind!" But she probably looks out the window, sees it is still raining, and concludes that she is "trapped" and can do nothing other than stay right there and try to keep from going out of her mind.

But is she really without alternatives? Not at all. She could, of course, abandon the children. She could simply take off and leave the children to whatever fate would dictate. And the objection is raised, "But she would never do that!" No, she probably would not. But it is an alternative, and at a particularly exasperating moment it may enter her mind. Chances are, however, that she does not allow herself to see it as a live option. Perhaps she does not trust herself enough to allow herself to say and accept it as a possibility that she could "just up and walk out." So she chooses not to recognize she has chosen not to leave.

There are very likely other alternatives for Marge, too, if she really examined the possibilities. Perhaps she could hire a baby-sitter and get away for a couple of hours, even if financial skimping were necessary in another area. Possibly a relative could come in for a while, or maybe she could combine children with a neighbor so they could give each other some escape. Perhaps she could bundle up all of them and herself and find a change of pace walking in the rain. The point is that we often avoid seeing the alternatives and then bemoan our helplessness and lack of choice. We are not trapped. Even the feeling of being trapped is a chosen feeling.

Suppose we do allow ourselves to recognize we have more freedom than we thought. How will we use that freedom? The most satisfying answer to this appears to be that our freedom is best used when we choose to live more spontaneously.

This idea has been variously described. Some have called it the inner-directed life in contrast to the outer-directed life. Others speak of self-actualizing. Perhaps it can be described by saying that as we move in the direction of living spontaneously we will become more aware of and more responsive to our inner impulses, feelings, needs, and self-chosen values. While we will be even more realistically aware of those around us, our responses will not be dictated by the desires or demands of others. We will respond in the way in which we choose. One mark of the spontaneous life is that it is lived in the present time, not the past or the future.

## Living in the Past

Many people live largely in the past. This often takes the form of remorse, regret, or bitterness. Some who have been exposed to punitive forms of religion may become "stuck" at the level of feeling perpetually guilty about things that have occurred in the past. They never feel they have been forgiven, because they cannot forgive themselves. It is too good to be true to believe that others or even God could forgive them. With these unresolved, pervasive feelings of guilt the individual keeps himself "unfree" to experience and enjoy the freedom to live *now*.

Another variation of living in the past is that of

feeling so inexorably in the grips of past events that one is unable to be a freely choosing person in the present. Of course there is some truth in this, which makes it possible to kid ourselves in this way. We unquestionably have some limitations that come to us from the past. We have been born with varying degrees of intellectual, physical, and emotional capabilities. Life's experiences up to this moment have affected us in various ways. Some of our capabilities may have been dulled. But with the possible exception of those who have been so badly damaged by hereditary or environmental factors that they can hardly be described as human, we have so much more capability in intellectual, physical, and emotional spheres than we ever choose to use that we cannot be described as trapped. In other words, despite whatever limitations to our free will we may have from a philosophical point of view, we are all surrounded by a vast territory in which we are free to move, the limits of which we never begin to explore.

Psychological insights about the development of human personality provide many people with another popular way of living in the past. For example, there will surely be some reader of this book who will become bogged down in the passages that describe childhood rejection and the problems that result. They will say, "Yes, that's me. That describes what happened to me." But instead of following up on this potentially freeing glimpse into their lives by asking themselves "How is this affecting me right now, and what can I do about it?" they will tend to go no further than to feel bitterness toward their parents, who led them to feel rejected, and helplessness about doing anything about themselves now.

It is well to recognize that psychotherapists have

sometimes unwittingly contributed to this problem by focusing too much on past experience. One of the legitimate criticisms of classical psychoanalysis, for example, is that it encourages the individual in analysis to dredge up every possible childhood memory and whenever feasible to see a causal relationship between those experiences and the individual's problems. While many people have undoubtedly been helped in analysis, this method of therapy is not only unnecessarily time-consuming, but it encourages the individual to focus on the past rather than on the present. Some clients of this and similar approaches to therapy have unquestionably capitalized on this opportunity to make a way of life out of constantly analyzing their past. Thus they manage to avoid dealing fully with their awareness of themselves and those around them in the present moment of their existence.

A more useful approach to therapy appears to be one in which the therapist, by means of his alertness to what is going on each moment within himself, confronts his clients with these awarenesses and thereby enables them to become more self-aware. When memories of significant past experience or past feelings intrude into this process of becoming self-aware, then these feelings can be taken as indications of unfinished business and can be dealt with as part of the current experience. For example, in one session a client named Ron expressed some anger toward his therapist for seeming to be indifferent toward him. Almost immediately Ron expressed the feeling that the therapist was condemning him for getting angry, "just as my father would have." The therapist knew that he felt neither indifferent nor condemning, so he encouraged Ron to talk to his father as though he were present in the room. In the "conversation" that followed, in which Ron alternately took the role of himself and his father, some of his still present feelings of anger and frustration—unfinished business of the past—were experienced and expressed. Out of many such moments in therapy Ron was able gradually to deal more directly and realistically in the present moment with his encounters with others (including the therapist), having less need to distort the present reality to make it conform with unresolved experiences from the past.

A discussion of living in the past cannot be concluded without mentioning the tendency of some to avoid the present by looking back to some glorious moment or period of the past.

The middle-aged former high school or college football star may still be cutting off tackle for long gainers in his fantasy. The aging beauty queen may be trying to appear twenty-two rather than experiencing her potential beauty and self-worth in the present moment. The evangelist may constantly relive and retell the experience of that moment when he was "saved from a life of sin" twenty years ago. The war veteran may dwell on the danger, excitement, and adventure he experienced in some far-off place and completely dull himself to the potential adventure available now.

## Living for the Future

Just as some people live primarily in the past, others avoid the present by living in the future. Some of us spend most of our time getting ready to do something. Perhaps we say, "Someday I'm going to spend a whole summer traveling through Europe." But always we manage to find "good and sufficient reasons" why *now* is not the time to do it. Perhaps we manage this by making "The Plan" so grandiose and unrealistic that excuses for postponing its fulfillment will always seem overwhelming.

One single, elementary schoolteacher had the dream, as she put it, of "going to Ireland to find a leprechaun." She sold her home and, to the expressed dismay of a number of friends and relatives, took part of the proceeds and went one summer to Ireland. She reported on her return that she had not completely found her "leprechaun." She discovered, for example, that she could sometimes be lonely and depressed even in that exquisitely beautiful and mystical country. But at least she did not live out her years in the frustrated thought that she could be happy if she could just get to the "promised land."

One man describes his father as a "sometime guy." "His whole life revolved around this word of his," says the son. "When I was a child he started to add a room to the house, and he's still living in that house with the skeleton of a room attached, which he is going to finish 'sometime.'"

Probably all of us live in the future to some extent. Often it takes the form of doing more planning and more organizing than we need to do. We spend the time *now* planning the things we will do for the coming week. When the time comes to do what we planned we no longer feel free to let ourselves be aware of whether that is really what we want to do at that moment. So we keep ourselves in a constant state of planning or fulfilling plans and leave ourselves little room to be open and responsive to our feelings of the moment. It is no wonder we sometimes feel trapped when we work so hard at it.

*Living Now!*

So to live spontaneously is to live—not in the past, not in the future—but now. It means being sensitive and responsive to our own selves. But for many people any movement in the direction of spontaneity must be preceded by a rediscovery of the capacity to be self-aware, since many of us have become virtually dead to the self.

One man, Jack, who grew up in a religiously oriented home where he gained the impression that he must always be totally unselfish and subjugate any of his desires to those of everyone around him, tells how he woke up the morning after his first visit to a psychotherapist and broke into tears, sobbing for forty-five minutes or an hour. In describing the feeling that he had that morning, he says, "Somehow that therapist got through to me the fact that I have a self—a self that is separate from anyone else. And it was such a new and reassuring idea to me that I couldn't stop crying from the relief I felt." It is not surprising that Jack, like many others, had to go through a considerable retraining effort to become sensitively aware of his feelings. All of his childhood training had been in the other direction. He had been taught to be sensitively aware of and responsive to the needs and desires of others and to turn off any awareness of his own desires, which would automatically be regarded as selfish and therefore sinful.

The lack of self-awareness often takes the form of deadness to feelings that are unacceptable and frightening to us. This would probably account, for example, for the almost total absence of enjoyable sexual sensation of some men and women. The same would be true of the individual whose anger never comes into focus, or the one whose anger has a long fuse, so that awareness always comes some time later when the anger-producing situation, along with the opportunity for expressing the anger, has become past history. It is not mental slowness but emotional slowness that prevents us from thinking until it is too late of just the right angry words we would have "liked" to have been able to say at the right moment.

## Listening to One's Self

Helping individuals recapture self-awareness is often one of the most useful services the competent therapist can provide. It seems likely, however, that the person who is not seriously emotionally damaged can make considerable progress without such help. It involves learning to listen to one's self—not shutting out those signals we have become accustomed to ignoring. Often a good way to start is to allow the simplest physical feelings to come through. Our bodies may be "aware" when we do not let our minds perceive. In an awkward social situation, for example, our legs may tense up when we are frightened and want to run even though we have suppressed the fear from conscious awareness.

Here again a group of intimates can be invaluable. If there are those with whom we can develop sufficient confidence that we can increasingly be ourselves, it will be surprising to us how quickly we can learn to be aware of a wealth of various feelings we have hitherto suppressed. This is one of the values of group psychotherapy in the professional setting, but the experience need not be limited to therapy groups.

Increasing self-awareness opens the door to the possibility of living more spontaneously, but the result is by no means automatically achieved. As we have seen, the possibility of freedom is frightening to us and we build many defenses against the spontaneous life. We

may busy ourselves compulsively and develop meaningless rituals to occupy our hours and limit our opportunity for spontaneity; or we may live by rules and
put more emphasis than is necessary on the need for
self-control; or we may make love seem like slavery.

To begin to give up these defenses is frightening,
because they take most of the ambiguity out of life
and help us keep life cut and dried and our response
to life's situations predictable. We know pretty much
what we will do. Our lives are full of activity, the rules
are laid out, and we are in tight control of ourselves
most of the time.

## Legalism

But we pay a price for it all. Life loses much of its
color, its adventure, and its satisfactions in relationships when it is lived in these terms. Take legalism, for
example. The church, though it has no exclusive do-
main on legalism, provides many examples of people
who are essentially legalists.

A certain Mrs. Smith gained considerable prestige
and power in her denomination. This was largely because she was a tireless and efficient worker for the
church since her husband, a successful businessman,
had died and left her financially independent while
she still had many active years left. She devoted them
mainly to the church. She was also, of course, in a position to make large donations to her favorite projects
in the denomination, which did not diminish her influence among denominational leaders.

Mrs. Smith wore her increasing stature in the
church well. Correctness in behavior was important to
her, and she was every inch the "gracious lady." She
was charming and friendly. She did not throw her
weight around in any obvious fashion. If she had any

"secret sins" they were well hidden, and everyone would have been greatly surprised had any come to light. In spite of her friendliness and her habit of befriending many younger people, however, it would have been hard to have imagined her to be very close to anyone. She was the patroness of many, the confidante of none.

Not too long after the death of her husband, a minister came to the local church of which she was a member. She appeared to develop a deep respect, perhaps even affection, for this man, who had great talents. Toward the end of his ministry in that parish the relationship between Mrs. Smith and the minister, while still cordial, seemed perceptibly more distant, a fact that was puzzling to the minister.

When the minister had been in another church in the denomination for some time, his name began to appear as a candidate for various positions of importance within the church on the basis of his demonstrated abilities. But it also became apparent that his name was being dropped from consideration each time it came up. It eventually came to him through friends that there was a persistent rumor from a reliable source that he had had a sexual affair with one of the women of his former parish. With characteristic directness he traced the rumor to its source, the church's wealthy benefactress. When he confronted her, Mrs. Smith admitted that she was responsible for the rumor, although, as she said, "There may have been one or two others who thought the same thing." She said she was convinced that what she had reported was true and that she felt it was her duty to prevent such a person from achieving eminence in the church. Even if he were innocent, she felt, the fact that he could bring on such suspicion by his actions indicated he was a person of questionable judgment.

Though the minister had traced the rumor, he was only able in a small way to lessen its harmful effect on his career. It seems almost irrelevant to report that he had not been sexually involved with the woman in question though it had been a deeply significant relationship for him and filled a need for emotional intimacy he had not experienced elsewhere.

The wealthy widow serves as an example of the essential barrenness of the legalistic approach to life. True intimacy was unquestionably frightening to Mrs. Smith, and living life by the "rules" protected her from it. In a very practiced and not unpleasing way she was proper and friendly. Always the friendliness was within bounds. To have revealed enough of herself to have been emotionally close to another would probably have seemed like an impropriety to her. It is probable that her adherence to the rules made it difficult, if not impossible, to see herself clearly. No doubt *she* was sexually attracted to the minister, but this would be so untenable a thought that she would not allow herself to feel it. Perhaps she was faced with some brief doubts when faced with the decision as to whether or not to betray her "friend." But this was no doubt quickly, if sadly, resolved by her dedication to the rules. So it became her Christian duty to pass on her "knowledge" to others, and she willingly became judge, jury, and executioner.

Is there no place for rules in life? Yes, of course there is. Society provides many examples. We agree that we will drive on one side of the street rather than on the other and thus eliminate mass chaos. In a complex society we need such rules. And no doubt we have a responsibility to ourselves to see that helpful ones are enacted and that destructive or overly restrictive laws are not enacted, or, if they have been enacted, to see that they are repealed. But when rules become a way of life, they become a problem. When we constantly judge ourselves and other people good or bad, the rules become distancing devices. We tend to classify people, including ourselves; and we give up our freedom to accept, enjoy, and respond to people, including ourselves, as they are.

## The Hierarchy of "Sins"

Almost always in rule-dominated lives, a hierarchy of "sins" tends to develop, and those "sins" we tend to find most frighteningly desirable but unacceptable in ourselves tend to head the list. We are likely to be most condemning of "sins of passion"—expressions of anger, sexual desire or activity, unrestrained expressions of love and warmth, unconfined creative thinking that threatens changes in the established order.

Far down on the list and sometimes the subject of polite discussion but never accorded the passionate condemnation given the first order of "sins" are such things as indifference, coldness, prejudice, unscrupulous business practices, hypocrisy, judgmentalism, and the like. Of these we tend to be tolerant, for this, as we say, is "just the way people are"!

Becoming less legalistic helps us to live more spontaneously. It will also help us if we move beyond self-control into a more creative relationship with ourselves. Many of us have deep-seated fears that if we allow ourselves to be responsive to our impulses and desires, we will in one way or another "run amuck" and be destructive to those about us and perhaps ultimately to ourselves. Because of this pervasive mistrust of ourselves, we feel it necessary to clamp lids of self-control on our lives. We set up a kind of inner board of censorship through which most of our impulses to act or speak must pass and be voted upon before action can be permitted. Obviously, much of our potential spontaneity is lost in the process.

## Beyond Self-control

It is, therefore, inevitable that the question "Is there a need for self-control?" arises when a way of life is being espoused that encourages freedom of thought and action. And it is vital that no glib, easy answer be given, for it is an important question with many ramifications.

Situations do exist where it can be said without equivocation "Yes, do exercise self-control." When, for example, individuals have the desire to destroy the life or property of others or when they have the urge to take their own lives or act in obviously self-destructive ways, it is important that they control these impulses. Society has found it necessary and desirable, when it has the opportunity, to impose control on such persons by limiting their freedom by restraining them. (It is possible, however, that good arguments exist for granting the person the right to choose to take his own life in certain instances as, for example, in incurable illness where there is great pain or burden on the lives of others.)

One of the most painful tragedies in American life today is the suicides that occur among high school and college students—frequently those of great promise. It could not be said too strongly to them, "Please, please, hold on! Life may often seem painful and meaningless. Perhaps you feel suddenly and terribly disillusioned. But at least bear with the struggle and give yourselves the perspective of a few more years before you make such an irrevocable decision."

It is not enough simply to develop self-control, even though we may need to use it to curb destructive impulses. The ultimately satisfying answer is to deal effectively with problems that underlie our destructive impulses so that we can move beyond the need for self-control. The basic problem is self-hate, for self-destructiveness and destructiveness directed toward others go hand in hand. The nation, for example, that sets out to destroy other nations (i.e., Hitler's Germany) is bent on a self-destructive course. The man who has the urge to rape women and who follows his impulses is not benefitting himself at the expense of another, he is destroying himself. And, of course, his self-hate is also evident in the obvious lack of confidence in his ability to relate to women in ways that would be more satisfying both to them and to himself. The man who beats his wife is not acting in his own self-interest, for he will not achieve a deeply satisfying relationship thereby. And the wife who withholds affection and sexual intercourse from her husband as a way of punishing him is punishing herself as well.

So let us be very clear about one thing. The violent or destructive acts we are so often afraid we will do if we do not control ourselves are not the result of true freedom or spontaneity. The murderer is not free. He is an enslaved, tormented person who is driven by pent-up feelings of self-hate that have been projected outward onto other individuals or onto society at large. The superheated steam of this hatred builds up in his internal pressure cooker until whatever self-control he possesses is bypassed in an explosion of violence. To exhort such a person to "control himself" may be a necessary stop-gap measure, although it is likely to be futile. Any thorough-going help must deal with the man's self-hate.

Most of us may feel some impulses within ourselves to be destructive to others or to ourselves, which we sense the need to curb by self-control. Often the inner pressure is not too great and we can be successful in this control if we choose to go that route, but the more such self-control we need to impose on ourselves the less able we will be to be carefree and spontaneous. And spontaneity is a deliciously desirable way of living.

It will be a far more freeing experience if we can discover why we feel destructive and through this exploration reduce the self-hate to the point where we have relatively little need for self-control. A professional therapist can often be very helpful here, for he can provide a relatively secure environment where hatreds (both toward the self and others) can be expressed and explored with a minimum of danger. Often in therapy people discover that they are not nearly as "dangerous" to themselves or others as they feared. They find they had been so frightened of freedom that they had imagined themselves far more potentially harmful than they were as a way of keeping themselves rigidly controlled.

## Love and Freedom

Another vital question remains to be discussed in regard to living spontaneously. Can we be deeply involved in a love relationship and still be free to be spontaneous?

A great many people act as though love and spontaneity are incompatible. There are two frequent feelings that contribute to this reaction that love and freedom cannot coexist. And, of course, they help to make love that much more frightening to us.

One of these feelings has to do with the idea that the revealing of ourselves, which intimacy involves, gives the other person power over us, thereby limiting our freedom to do what we want to do. John, a man in his thirties, had been seeing a psychotherapist for a number of weeks, having been ordered to do so by a judge as a condition of probation following conviction on charges of homosexual involvement with three eleven- and twelve-year-old boys. As far as surface indications were concerned, John seemed cooperative with this program and even eager to secure help for his problem. He showed up regularly and on time for his appointments. He showed no obvious reluctance to talk about his problems and other relevant information about his past. And yet the therapist gradually felt a growing restlessness and frustration in his relationship with John. Finally, as his own feelings became more apparent to him, he said to him, "You know, John, I don't think we're really getting through to each other. I guess it's your eyes that bother me the most. The feeling is hard to describe, but it's almost as if there were an invisible wall between your eyes and mine—a wall that has never been absent in all the time we've been talking together."

There was a considerable pause before the young man replied, "I guess I know what you're talking about. I realize I'm on guard. I have the feeling I can never let anyone see me completely—know all about me. It would give the other person too many strings on me. I'm afraid I would become his puppet."

John and the therapist discussed this theme at length, and it is not surprising to know that he had had these same feelings in relationship with his par-

ents—and particularly his mother—during his childhood years. He had developed the defense of withdrawing into himself and permitting his parents to
see as few of his real feelings as possible as a way of
avoiding manipulation by them. The feeling persisted
even when he was an adult and quite capable of deciding his own courses of action. He still felt that he
would be helpless to avoid being manipulated if he
allowed others to really know him.

The other feeling that leads us to shy away from
love because it appears to threaten our freedom is
probably even more common. This is the idea that love
is inescapably tied up with obligation and responsibility. Among other ways in which this duty theme
operates is the idea that if we really love another we
will cease doing what we want to do and concentrate
on pleasing the one we love. Such feelings often strike
a death blow to the experience and expression of love.
In family life, for example, we often talk and think a
great deal about the responsibilities involved. Men talk
about their lack of freedom to do what they would
like to do because of the necessity of providing adequately for their families. So work becomes a noxious,
tolerated duty. And to hear many wives talk one would
think, perhaps, rightly, that their whole lives revolve
around feelings reflected in such statements as "Fred
wouldn't like it if I did this or didn't do that," or, "I'd
really like to join you, Helen, but the children have to
come first, you know."

So all of life becomes hedged about with responsibilities and the necessity of pleasing others "brought
about" by love. And virtually everything in life, from
daily work, fidelity, sexual intercourse, and "second
honeymoons" to family picnics, walking in the park,
and holding hands in the movie, becomes a dutiful and

essentially joyless act that we do in hope that spouse and children will be pleased. It is no wonder that love, when approached this way, seems like slavery and a many "unsplendored" thing!

It is not surprising that when so many people view love this way that a "playboy (and playgirl) philosophy" would develop in our culture in which physical intimacy without emotional intimacy would become very attractive to us as a way of life. The essential message of the philosophy seems to be, "As long as I can remain indifferent to my sexual partners I can retain my freedom and individuality. Once I begin to allow myself to care for someone, I've had it! I'm on my way to becoming a slave." The joker in this deck is that the moment we embrace this philosophy we have walked out on the freedom to have the most deeply satisfying fun of all—a love relationship freely experienced and expressed.

The basic problem underlying our feeling that love and freedom are incompatible is our old nemesis, self-hate. We assume, and often we have been taught to assume, that if we act freely and do what we want to do we will destroy relationships that are important to us. But this involves a colossal distrust of ourselves. We are, in effect, saying to ourselves, "You are such a miserable creature and so self-destructive that if you do not watch yourself carefully you will alienate everyone you care for and end up all alone."

The reality is that one of the quickest ways of alienating another person is to put every effort into pleasing them. When we try to put their wishes foremost, we are likely to become a nonentity in their eyes. It is not particularly pleasing to attempt to relate to a person who has no apparent desires of his own, who always bends to accommodate our wishes, and who makes an uncomplaining doormat of himself for us to walk upon. Furthermore, when we deny our own desires and put such emphasis on pleasing the other person, we quickly come to resent that person for "taking advantage of us." That resentment will then likely be expressed in any number of ways. Perhaps we begin to take on a martyr posture and express by word or attitude the feeling: "After all I've done for you, the least you could do would be to try to please *me* once in a while."

It is much more straightforward and ultimately satisfying to be what we want to be and do what we want to do. As we learn that we can value ourselves and respond to our own desires, it is unlikely we will act in ways that destroy relationships with those for whom we care—because this will be destructive toward ourselves, too. It is true that more flare-ups of disagreement and anger may occur, because our wishes and those of others will not always agree, but two individuals in this situation are likely to respect each other for being sufficiently independent to express feelings openly, and the way is then clear to battle through to some agreement.

If we do find ourselves acting in ways that constantly hurt those we love and destroy our relationships with them it would be advisable to seek professional help, for it would be an indication that we have so much self-hate that we have a need to hurt ourselves, since hurting others is self-destructive.

The early Christian Augustine is said to have given the advice "Love God and do as you please." This is a profound idea, but it can be carried an additional step and be made to read "Love yourself and do as you please," for if you truly value yourself, you will not hurt people unnecessarily. To do so would be to hurt yourself.

This seems too good to be true to most of us. We are so convinced that to live spontaneously is to live dangerously toward others and ourselves, but if we can begin, perhaps a little at a time, to be more responsive to our inner selves, we will discover that living spontaneously is exciting and rewarding to ourselves and to those we care for. Once having made that discovery we will not be content with less than an ever-increasingly spontaneous life.

XVII

## LOVING AND TREMBLING

TED, A MAN IN his middle twenties, sought the help of a psychotherapist because he was having difficulty in his marriage. One week, after he had had several sessions with the therapist, sudden and dramatic changes occurred in his relationship with his wife, Patti.

Both of them began to talk to each other about events and feelings that they had never discussed before. In some ways it was an agonizing week for them. Anger that had been pent up for months, and even years, poured forth. In the course of their self-disclosures each of them revealed that they had had brief sexual "flings" with another since their marriage. More expressions of anger and hurt burst forth, reaching an intensity they had never experienced before. But when the anger and hurt had been expressed other feelings began to manifest themselves. They became aware that they felt closer and more sexually alive to each other than they ever had before. As they moved toward each other they found themselves exquisitely sensitive to each other's touches and caresses.

Sexual intercourse had always been marred for the couple by the fact that Ted invariably had his orgasm almost immediately after entering the vagina, leaving both Patti and himself feeling frustrated and cheated. Now, suddenly, this, too, was changed. To his amazement he found that during intercourse he now remained for many minutes at the peak of the most delicious sexual enjoyment he had ever experienced, yet he was not aware of making any effort to control the timing of his sexual climax, but was caught up completely in the enjoyment of his own sensations and Patti's obvious enjoyment.

All of this occurred in one week between Ted's sessions with the therapist. When he appeared for his next hour it was natural that he describe what had happened. He did so with great enthusiasm, but then he said, "It was such a great week that I just can't understand what happened to me today. I discovered that my hands were literally shaking, and I just felt scared to death."

Ted's bewilderment was understandable. He assumed that he would feel more confident because of his new-found ability to be more completely himself and more expressive of his love and his sexual desire. The last thing he expected of himself was that he would become very frightened. He did not reckon with his fear of love, which he has in common with the rest of us.

Time and again experiences such as this confirm that we are most frightened by that for which we most long—the experience of intimacy. What can we do about this fear of love, which so often confronts us in ourselves and in those we love?

Perhaps one of the most helpful things we can do about it is to become clearly aware of it. Our relationships would often be more understandable if we could see these fears clearly in ourselves and others. For example, couples frequently report sequences of events in which they first felt very close and then shortly thereafter began arguing or nagging one another about some seemingly insignificant thing. These experiences mystify them and often lead to doubts about their love for each other. It would be helpful if we could recognize that for most of us the exquisite experience of intimacy is a razor's edge, which we cannot allow to exist for more than a few moments. When intimacy does occur, then we frequently trump up some "reason" for moving away from it.

In other instances we prevent ourselves from even momentary experiences of intimacy by finding something (almost anything!) to be angry, hurt, irritated, nervous, or busy about any time love comes threateningly close.

Anna, a woman in her early forties who was seeing a psychotherapist, followed a constant pattern for many weeks in her sessions. It would often be obvious during her weekly hour that she had some inclination to respond to the feelings of warmth and acceptance that he felt for her. Invariably, however, toward the end of the session she would find some reason to become violently angry with him. She would read some manipulative or rejecting meaning into some innocuous statement or glance of his. She would then explode at him, accuse him of being a phony and a charlatan, and stomp out of the room after hurling all manner of invectives at him. On one occasion when she was angry she refused to leave; and it was necessary for him to call the police to force her to do so.

But some dogged persistence in Anna kept her coming back week after week. And despite the anger that her behavior aroused in the therapist, which frequently led him to shout back and threaten never to see her again, he allowed the appointments to continue. Finally, after the pattern of her behavior had been pointed out many times, Anna gradually became aware of the fact that she was desperately frightened of caring. She began to recognize that she had to reject and hurt anyone who gave evidence of caring for her lest she be caught in the trap of the vulnerability of caring and be hurt again as she had been hurt many times before. Once this awareness began to dawn on her, Anna's moments of anger toward the therapist became less frequent, less violent, and more quickly over and done with when they did occur.

Gaining awareness of our fear of love is often a difficult task, for we tend to disguise it from ourselves and others by employing many defenses against intimacy.

One man, Bill, invariably sounded angry in any discussion with his wife. The two of them had been seeing a marriage counselor together for a number of sessions. During these sessions the two of them often clashed, and the arguments frequently seemed to start because Bill sounded so angry. Finally the therapist became suspicious of this, and when the husband spoke out loudly and with apparent anger toward his wife, the therapist interrupted to ask, "Bill, are you really angry right now?" Bill replied that he was not. "You sound as though you are." To this remark Bill replied, "I'm just speaking positively and with conviction. I'm not mad."

It appeared on further exploration that Bill was often not angry when he sounded as though he were. Perhaps he did have a reservoir of hostility built up over the years that had something to do with this behavior, but the function that it appeared to serve in relation to his wife and other people he cared for was one of keeping it virtually impossible to experience intimacy.

There are many similar defenses against intimacy. We may keep people at a distance by seeming indifferent to them, by being rigid or legalistic, or by playing the role of martyr. As long as we are successful at employing these ways of keeping others away, it is hard for us to become aware of our fear of love, for we make the possibility of intimacy so remote that there is little "danger" of our experiencing it. With the lion so successfully caged, we do not become aware of our fear of it!

## Recognizing Our Fear of Love

If we can begin to see what we are doing and begin to give up some of our defenses, then we will be more likely to experience our fear of love directly. Once this occurs we are in a much better position to do something about it. It will also be helpful if we cannot only be aware of our fear of love, but also accept it both in ourselves and in others. Here, as elsewhere, caring for ourselves seems to be the starting point for personality growth.

If we can experience and accept our fear of love, we will have less need of indirect ways of expressing it, which are almost invariably harmful to relationships. Instead of finding some pretext for withdrawing when we experience more intimacy than our fear will permit, we can admit our fear to ourselves and often to the other person as well. This direct way of responding to our fear will be far less destructive to the relationship. A natural ebb and flow of the experience and expression of love will then be possible, as we experience such intimacy as we are ready for and then withdraw for a time as our fear asserts itself too strongly. As we see this pattern clearly we will be far more able to take in stride apparent setbacks in our associations with others.

It also makes a big difference when we can recognize that when someone we love acts destructively or hurtfully toward us it is almost certainly an indication that he, too, is afraid rather than that he does not care for us. We may be just as hurt or express as much anger as we would if we did not have this insight. The chances of resolving the situation are much better, however, because we ourselves will not be likely to react as though we have been completely rejected and unloved. This is when we often play that "he loves me, he loves me not" game in which we tally up what we consider to be indications of how the other person feels about us. Often our feelings of worth become involved, as we say to ourselves, "There must be something the matter with me or he wouldn't treat me this way."

This game is pointless, for the problem does not usually lie in the absence of caring but rather in the fear of love, which leads the person to act as though he does not care. Of course, recognizing the existence of the fear of love does not always lead to a resolution of interpersonal difficulties. A woman, for example, might see that her husband belittles her constantly as a means of avoiding intimacy and as a way of coping with his own self-hate. Yet if she saw no crack in the wall of this defense, she might ultimately come to the conclusion that it would be self-destructive for her to continue the marriage. And a child might still have to be taken from a cruel father even though it might be recognized that his brutality is rooted in a terrible fear of love.

It will also be helpful if we can discover that the

potential hurt of not experiencing and expressing love ultimately far outweighs the risks that accompany intimacy. We can never eliminate the possibility that we will be hurt when we dare to love. The emotional involvement of caring always includes vulnerability; in fact we can be certain that we will sometimes be hurt if we allow ourselves to love. Someone we love will die; someone we love will be injured; someone we love will be incurably and painfully ill; someone we love will be so frightened and mistrustful of our caring that they will react in ways that are hurtful or even destructive to us.

These are painful experiences, and we cannot avoid them if we choose to love. It is part of the human dilemma that love always includes the element of hurt. We are invariably hurt by those we love, and, as the song has it, "You always hurt the one you love, the one you shouldn't hurt at all." So it is not surprising that we are frightened of love and tend to shy away from it. The self-disclosure and involvement of love is a sometimes painful joy.

What are the alternatives to a life in which love is experienced and expressed? Does such a life hold out the hope of any less hurt? Only two other alternatives appear to be available. One would be, if it is possible, to cut oneself off completely from the experience of love. Such a person would say in effect to themselves, "I won't allow anyone to mean anything to me. I may have business relationships of one kind or another, but no one will be important to me beyond the immediate dealings in which we find each other useful, and no one will learn anything of a personal nature about how I feel or who I really am. I'll never allow myself to experience the desire or need for love." Perhaps this kind of life could be achieved, but it sounds like a desperately lonely existence. Perhaps a person could keep so busy or be so controlled that he could even block the loneliness out of awareness, but what kind of life is that? The viewpoint suggested here does, of course, involve a value judgment that meaningfulness is found above all else in human relationships, although it does appear that few of us would *choose* to live so isolated an existence.

The other alternative is more often practiced, but it seems almost equally unsatisfying. This way of life would be to love guardedly and almost secretly. Although he may not be aware of it, such a person says to himself, "All right, so I admit *to myself* that I care for my children and my wife. And maybe there are a few other people in the world who mean something to me. But I'm going to play it cool. I'll never reveal too much of myself or let them know how much I care. No sense getting too far out on a limb or being too enthusiastic about our relationship. No use letting them see how much they mean to me. They'd be likely to find some way of using it to push me around or hurt me." A lot of us settle for this approach to love. But this, too, makes for a kind of loneliness and cheats us out of the deepest and most satisfying experiences of love. And since it involves a guardedness and calculated dullness in our relationships, it cheats us of the free, unburdened feeling that spontaneity in our actions and words could give us. All of life becomes toned down and the exhilarating excitement is taken away.

The risks of love are ever-present, but the alternatives are not inviting. So from the standpoint of satisfying living it *is* better even "to have loved and lost than never to have loved at all."

## Taking a Chance on Love

If we postponed the experience and expression of love until we no longer feared it, we would postpone it forever. Some people do appear to use their fear of love as a perpetual excuse for stalemated living—loving and trembling seem to go together. If we desire love we must learn to love in spite of our fears.

This process of "taking a chance on love" might be compared to the experience of a person who wants to make parachute jumps. If he is not a fool, he is frightened. And no amount of prejump training will eradicate that fear. When the time comes to make the leap he will be trembling internally and, quite possibly, externally. No amount of reassurance by experienced jumpers will make it otherwise. Making the leap of love is not too unlike this. No amount of advance preparation or reassurance from others will keep us from experiencing fear. It is different, however, in that we can make some tentative leaps in the direction of self-disclosure and the involvement of love and withdraw back into the security of emotional distance if the experience is too frightening. The parachutist, once committed, doesn't have that option!

When we make our first moves toward deeper experiences and more open expressions of love, it may seem at first that our fear is greatly intensified. This is a very critical time, for we may become so frightened that we choose to withdraw permanently and not allow ourselves another chance to feel so deeply.

This sometimes happens in psychotherapy. After a few sessions a person may begin to respond to the therapist's warmth with feelings of caring. Perhaps the individual does not even allow himself to verbalize these feelings but suddenly "discovers" he cannot afford the sessions or does not have sufficient time to work them into a busy schedule.

It is understandable that the experience of fear is intensified at first when we allow ourselves to love more deeply. In the past our defenses—the devices we used to keep ourselves emotionally distant from others —protected us not only from the experience of love but also from the full awareness of our fear. As we allow the defenses to crumble we stand naked and vulnerable before our fear.

One thing that will help as we begin to allow ourselves the experience of love will be the awareness that we are no longer in the same circumstances as we were when the fear of love developed within us. When we were first exposed to the risks of love, we were children. And when we experienced the hurts of feeling rejected, we were relatively helpless to do anything about the situation. No wonder we were frightened and built whatever defenses against hurt we could by walling ourselves off emotionally.

## We Aren't Helpless

Often as adults we still feel helpless, as though we were still children. But we are not helpless. If we express love and are rejected, we can do something about it—we can express our anger and frustration. If our loving proves unsatisfying we can withdraw from that person if we choose to and express our love to others more able to respond. We can also discover that another person's inability to express love to us when we love them has nothing to do with our value as a person. Perhaps most important of all we can learn that we can survive hurt and that, while it is never pleasant, it need not be catastrophic.

Our fear of love will never completely disappear any more than would the fear of the parachutist. In both instances there is always a realistic risk of hurt, but as we are able to enter into more and more emotionally intimate relationships, the fear will gradually lessen.

We will learn from experience that the satisfactions far exceed the occasional hurts we experience, and we will have so much fun enjoying the intimacy and the freedom of spontaneous living, we will give decreasing attention to the hurts or our fear of them.

We will find it increasingly easy to be ourselves and to express all our feelings, for we will have increasing confidence that people will generally like us as we are. And when we are frightened, we will likely find it comfortable to express that feeling, too—and expressing it will help to dissipate it.

A sentence in the New Testament reads, "There is no fear in love, but perfect love casts out fear." (I John 4:18) It is true. There is no fear *in* love—only fear *of* love and the vulnerability it involves. And the repeated experience of love reduces fear.

Whether the central message of the New Testament, which revolves around the crucifixion of Jesus, is regarded as the literal truth or as a myth growing out of man's yearning for meaning in life, the theme is a deeply moving one. It is often garbled by theological lingo, but it finally comes down to relationships and appears to be essentially this: God risked creating persons so independent they could love him or thumb their noses at him. He went even further and chose to love them. As it always does, the decision to love necessarily included suffering. But it must have been worth the risk, for perhaps the alternative even for God was the ultimate loneliness of having no one to love.

We can discover for ourselves that it is worth the risk to love, even though we tremble and even though we know we will sometimes experience the hurt we fear.